Pendulum for Beginners

Unlocking the Secrets of Pendulums, Dowsing, Spiritual Healing, Magic, and Divination

Free Bonus from Silvia Hill available for limited time

Hi Spirituality Lovers!

My name is Silvia Hill, and first off, I want to THANK YOU for reading my book.

Now you have a chance to join my exclusive spirituality email list so you can get the ebooks below for free as well as the potential to get more spirituality ebooks for free! Simply click the link below to join.

P.S. Remember that it's 100% free to join the list.

~~$27~~ FREE BONUSES

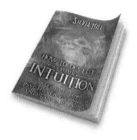

 9 Types of Spirit Guides and How to Connect to Them

 How to Develop Your Intuition: 7 Secrets for Psychic Development and Tarot Reading

 Tarot Reading Secrets for Love, Career, and General Messages

Access your free bonuses here
https://livetolearn.lpages.co/pendulum-for-beginners-paperback/

Table of Contents

Introduction

The pendulum has served as a tool for divination and dowsing rituals for thousands of years. Not only is it an incredible way to gain guidance in life, but it can also help locate resources, lost objects, and even people. Pendulums are considered one of the most utilized divinatory tools there is. Whether you're looking for simple yes/no answers to your questions, or a guided reading of your future, pendulums serve various purposes and are used in many rituals. Throughout history, pendulums have been used extensively and are now gaining attention again in the modern age. Their use is now accepted in numerous cultures and belief systems.

Although the pendulum is quickly gaining popularity, many people try using it briefly and then give up altogether. This is usually because they do not understand how to properly interpret pendulum readings and results. While using a pendulum seems simple in nature, you need patience, belief, knowledge, and, most of all, practice to get the best results. Once you're confident that a universal guide is working with you to give you answers, you'll start seeing viable results in no time.

This book is the perfect guide for your pendulum magic journey. Whether you want to learn about dowsing, healing magic, or divination rituals using pendulums, this book covers it all. Before we delve into pendulum rituals, it is important to understand where the concept of pendulums originated and when they began to be used for guidance purposes. To help you figure that out, the opening chapter of this book provides a detailed history of pendulums and their use through time so that you can begin your spiritual exploration journey on a solid basis.

Pendulums usually consist of a cone shape hung on a chain. Following that definition, anything can be a pendulum as long as one end of the chain is heavier and creates a swinging motion. There are various types of pendulums out there, each designed for special purposes, which will be discussed in detail in the upcoming chapters. Once you understand what type of pendulum you need for your ritual, you'll be ready to move on to the next part of the process. This will include cleansing and programming your pendulum to ensure no negative energies interfere and create an imbalance in your pendulum, thereby affecting the outcomes of your ritual.

In chapter 5, you'll be introduced to crystal pendulums and how to interpret their readings. After that, each chapter will define different pendulum magic rituals, including dowsing, divination, healing, balancing, intuition, and other magic rituals. There is also a chapter that provides detailed steps to make a pendulum chart for deeper readings and interpretations. Once you've gathered enough information about the specific process you plan to perform, all you need is a good pendulum that resonates with you and the intention to perform the ritual, which is the most important aspect of pendulum magic. If you're ready to explore this age-old instrument and discover how it can benefit you, by all means, keep reading!

Chapter 1: A Brief History of Pendulums

The opening chapter of this book is dedicated to pendulums and their use throughout history. Pendulums were traditionally used for a multitude of purposes, some of which are still applied today. Other practices related to this magical tool are fairly new. Dowsing is one of the most well-known applications of pendulums. However, there are plenty of other ways to incorporate this tool into your practice. To help you understand the concept behind their use, the following pages feature prime examples of how pendulums have helped people enhance this practice in both ancient and modern times.

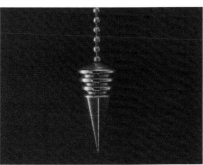

The key to choosing a pendulum is to find an object that lets the practitioner rely on their intuitive powers.

The Theory of Pendulum

A pendulum is a symmetrical, weighted tool attached to a single strand of cord or chain. Unlike similar magical objects, pendulums weren't made of metal or other magnetic materials. Instead, the item at the end of the cord was made from stone – usually a crystal with strong magical properties. These days, practitioners may also use metal balls, wooden beads, keys, and other trinkets of personal significance. Pendulums are used for spiritual guidance, to get answers to questions, to obtain help when making critical decisions, to cleanse your energy, and much more. Contemporary practitioners may also use it to find hidden objects, pets, and sources of illnesses or allergies in or near a person's body. Determining blockage, closing, or malfunction in your chakras (the body's primary energy centers) is another application of pendulum artistry used for healing purposes.

The key to choosing a pendulum is to find an object that lets the practitioner rely on their intuitive powers. The user can ask questions from their pendulum about the future or anything they may need guidance for. Holding the pendulum, they tap into their intuition. The object receives the information from the user's intuition, and by moving in a different direction, it lets the user know the answer to their question. It is believed that pendulums represent the physical manifestation of the user's soul, higher self, or, as it is called in modern times, their sixth sense. Pendulums can also help transmit information from spiritual guides, ancestors, and teachers.

Because it's a relatively simple tool, the question you ask your pendulum should also be simple. Beginners are generally advised to only ask questions that can be answered with a "yes" or "no." In contrast, advanced practitioners can also make more complex inquiries. Regardless of the complexity of the questions, they must be direct and backed up by strong intent. Pendulums connect the rational (conscious) side of the brain with the intuitive (subconscious) one, provided there is a powerful intent to do so on the rational side. When these two elements are connected, you can tap into your intuition and confidently make every decision – unlike when you rely only on the rational part of your mind.

That said, the artistry of pendulum use requires a little practice and plenty of trust in your gut instincts. People often believe that the tool only responds to the small movements of nerves in the practitioner's hand and nothing more. It may take opening one's mind to accept where the answers come from, especially if you also want to access information from other higher beings and not just your intuition.

What Is Dowsing?

Dowsing is an ancient divination form that uses tools like bobbers, Y rods, L rods, and pendulums. It's one of the simplest forms of divination using pendulums. The tools were traditionally made by the practitioner, although nowadays, you can buy them online or from any well-equipped shop selling magical supplies. In case you want to make your own tools, you'll also find plenty of information about it to help you out. That way, you'll feel more connected to your pendulum, which goes a long way in learning to rely on your intuition.

As with learning to use any other magical tool, mastering dowsing with pendulums requires grounding, focus, intention, intuitive listening skills, and practice. Practitioners typically learn dowsing by asking the pendulum simple and trivial questions. You definitely want to know more about tapping into your intuition before you place your future on the line. Typically, the user would seek an answer before deciding between two choices, so the pendulum would only confirm the answer from these two options. Depending on which way the pendulum swings, you can find answers to questions such as buying or selling something, spending money one way or another, moving or staying to live in one place, changing your job or not, etc.

How practitioners decipher their messages depends on how determined they are to see the pendulum's movements. For example, practitioners may interpret swinging in a clockwise direction as a "yes," and a simple left-to-right movement as a "no." Others may choose to see these responses the other way around. Even knowing that, at the beginning of your learning journey, you may get unclear answers, which is entirely normal – it simply means you'll have to practice some more. Practitioners also recommend honing one's grounding skills to obtain accurate information.

That said, no matter how you practice it, dowsing won't give you information as precise as the name of the person you'll meet any time from now or even the date you'll meet them. However, if you're making a decision about who to ask for help and you have two names in mind, the pendulum can help you pick the right person. Dowsing has also been used for developing one's intuition. It can help open the chakras, allowing the user to direct their energy through their body, manipulate it, and enhance it during magical practices or throughout life in general.

The History of Pendulum Practice

The practice of dowsing can be traced back to ancient times and is even recorded in the Bible. The earliest known pendulums were made from flexible papyrus fronds. The material allowed them to spin and sway at the same time. In the Bible, this motion has been described as rods being turned into serpents, showing the requested information with their slithering movements. One of the historical figures to have used this technique was Moses, who applied it to find water in the desert.

Historical evidence of dowsing with pendulums was documented in 400 BCE when the Pythian Oracle of Delphi applied this art to seek answers about the future. King Alfred the Great (848-899 AD) was fascinated by the practice of dowsing, and he immortalized it in the piece he commissioned to be made. The figure holds two objects (known as the Alfred Jewel) crossed and pointing in a direction that indicates answers. There are also records of pendulums being used in Ancient Rome and Egypt. A couple of centuries later, in the late 1500s, Italian scientist Galileo Galilei studied the art of pendulum use and made a report that many other European scientists took advantage of. One of these scientists was a polymath, Leonardo Davinci. Around the same time, Queen Elizabeth I became interested in dowsing, inviting several French and German dowsers to instruct her. This reportedly led to the development of copper and tin mining practices in Cornwall.

By the mid-1600s, dowsing was widely used to find lucrative mining places for precious metals, including gold. However, the practice also reached a point where the Catholic Church found it necessary to ban it. Although criticism directed toward pendulums and dowsing was nothing new (Pope John XXII had already declared its users to be witches in the 1300s), in the 17th century, it was associated with the occult and was labeled a diabolical practice along with several other witchcraft practices. While the allegations of the Church are still considered unfounded, it was enough to subdue pendulum dowsing for a while.

In 1833, French chemist Michel-Eugène Chevreul researched the pendulum's movement. He found that the tool actually moved due to the involuntary reflexes of the user's hand. This movement is known today as the "ideomotor reflex," triggered by subconscious thoughts and emotions, also known as intuition. Chevreul also established that the pendulum responds to the changes in a person's energetic field, representing the spiritual manifestation of their higher self and intuition. Once a piece of information leaves the hidden depths of the subconscious mind, this triggers a reflex in the practitioner's arm, moving the pendulum in their hand. This confirmed the theory that while the muscles and nerves move the arm, they could only do so due to the intuitive activity of the person's brain. After this discovery, the use of pendulums again started to gain popularity, and scientists took a renewed interest in studying how this magical tool harnesses information from one's intuition.

Abbe Mermet, a French priest, also took an interest in pendulums in the early 20th century. Inspired by the story of Moses, Mermet pioneered a pendulum to find water and minerals in the African deserts. He dowsed by swinging the pendulum over a map, relying on his intuition to find the object of his inquiries. Later, he was asked to find missing persons and was even commissioned by the Vatican to solve archaeological issues for the city-state. Mermet also dowsed for the location of illnesses or injuries in the human body, making him one of the pioneers of modern exploratory diagnostics. Although this practice is believed to have been used since ancient times, Mermet was honored for his work.

Dowsing was also used in World War II by Abbe Bouly, who served as an explorer for mines on the beaches of France. His efforts led to saving thousands of soldiers' lives, for which he was honored by Pope Pius XII. Around the same time, Alfred Bovis, a French food taster, developed the Bovis Biometer. This device measures the energy that radiates from objects. This device used to rate the vibrational energy of food was a pendulum made of quartz crystal, still used by modern food scientists.

In the 1950s, Evelyn Penrose used pendulum dowsing to communicate with animals to heal them and learn more about them.

Known today as "animal whisperers," this is another practice that has gained popularity in modern times. Penrose also used pendulums to help resolve water source issues that several governments faced during that time. In fact, she would often dowse over the map of a country in her home, and once she located water, she would visit the location she had found.

Ernest Hartmann was a notable pendulum dowser throughout the 20th century who was also involved in finding water. He became known for mapping out underground water lines and pointing out areas where no water could be found. He established that these areas were out of balance energy-wise and could potentially disrupt the entire environment surrounding them. Furthermore, 21st-century scientists have discovered that living in these areas harms people's health. This phenomenon was coined "geopathic stress."

Pendulums and dowsing can be used for many purposes, and modern applications are constantly being developed. Modern devices are often built to follow the same energetic principles as applied in dowsing. In the upcoming section, you'll see some of the ways pendulums can be used for contemporary purposes. However, the list of applications is still growing and is expected to keep growing.

Modern Uses for Pendulums

Pendulums remain powerful magical tools any contemporary practitioner can use for numerous purposes. Here are some ways pendulums are used in modern times.

Finding Lost Objects

To employ the pendulum to find lost belongings, pets, people, or a place to stay, practitioners often use it over maps. They lay the map out on a table and move the pendulum over it while asking the tool to show the direction in which what they need lies. They'll find the object in that direction depending on whether it swings east, north, south, or west. Next, the practitioners will narrow down the space on the map and ask the pendulum whether the object in question is found in a specific place. They can even follow up with more specific questions, like confirming the name of the street or shop where the object may be located.

Self-Improvement

Modern practitioners often use pendulums for guidance when making life-changing decisions. For example, a person seeking professional advancement may consult a pendulum about potential new jobs they can apply for. They can see which position would be the most fulfilling for them while helping them hone their skills or develop new ones. Pendulums typically confirm answers you are already contemplating – even if only subconsciously. At other times, the answers one gets from the pendulum can be rather surprising. Fresh college graduates who contemplate continuing their studies often check with their pendulum to see whether it's the right decision. Several cases have been recorded when the pendulum advised against this decision and pointed to either getting a job, traveling, or pursuing other adventures. In these cases, the graduates only wanted to continue their studies because they didn't consciously know what else to do and not because they found studying a rewarding way to spend their time. Bearing this in mind, their pendulum helped them find a more fulfilling path.

Improving Physical and Mental Health

Those struggling to get fit, lose weight, or simply improve their physical health can consult a pendulum to resolve their issues. For example, suppose a person is unsure which activity will help them achieve their goals. In that case, they can ask the pendulum about the benefits of different exercises. Pendulums can also help find ideal relaxation methods and ways to establish a healthy sleep pattern, diet, and lifestyle in general. It can also answer questions about improving cognitive functions, which is another great way to keep your mental health in check. Experienced practitioners know how to tune their bodies to the pendulum's movement, allowing them to use their bodies instead of a pendulum. They simply close their eyes and let their body sway towards or away from the object, symbol, or activity in question.

Emotional and Spiritual Growth

If a practitioner has trouble finding the appropriate way to express their emotions, the pendulum can show it to them. For example, if someone is used to expressing their strong feelings about a particular topic but isn't sure if they should, consulting a pendulum can advise them against forcefully voicing their opinion – but also encourage them to find other ways to articulate what's on their mind. Sometimes, the pendulum will tell a person to speak up rather than bottle up their emotions. This leads to a balanced emotional life and the acquisition of emotional control skills. Pendulums can also help locate new spiritual beliefs and ideologies you can identify with. Spirituality, as the expression of your soul's desires, is fertile ground for dowsing and other pendulum divination practices. When you find the belief that aligns with your values, a pendulum can give a clear answer regarding whether the belief in question is suitable.

Affirmation Practices

Pendulums are widely known for their use in modern affirmation practices. And it doesn't take much to get revealing answers. Typically, the practitioner will simply sit and repeat an affirmation similar to this one:

"I have a good life because I have everything I need – success, happiness, and prosperity in all areas that matter."

Even if the person hasn't got everything going on great for them at present, affirming it can help them manifest the desired state in the future. This is because the more they repeat the affirmative statement, the more it stays ingrained in their subconscious. Over time, the conscious mind takes over, encouraging the person to seek action that enables the success, happiness, and prosperity they've manifested. It often only takes finding what you truly love doing in life to achieve all three of the desired states. As it happens, pendulums can show you how to find the purpose that leads to this.

Creating Spaces

Creating or finding the most appropriate space for living or your business is another great example of pendulum artistry. From putting together timeless decor to allowing the energy to flow freely through your home, pendulums can show you everything you need to know about arranging your space. The same applies to plants and herbs in your garden. If you want to know which plants you should add to your garden to enrich your practices, you must ask the pendulum. Not only that, but it's also believed that pendulums can help you communicate with plants. This idea is rooted in the experiment performed by Cleve Backster in 1966. Backster was an expert in the field of lie detectors who accidentally discovered that plants can provide an emotional response when threatened with abuse. They can pick up human emotions and react to them accordingly. This is what pendulums enhance as well.

Influencing the Conscious through Magic

While the answers come from the subconscious, a person can direct their conscious mind to influence their subconscious in a direction that makes their desires come true. In other words, by impacting the conscious, you can also promote the manifestation of the desires hidden in your subconscious. Contemporary practitioners often use pendulums to uncover their desires and place them in their conscious minds. Some of the most common desires for people are:

- Loving, affectionate, and accepting relationships
- A vacation that allows for ultimate relaxation
- A safe and comfortable living space
- Lasting physical, mental and emotional health
- Financial, academic, and professional prosperity

Practitioners often find that what they are looking for typically falls into these categories, even if they weren't aware of this. It's not uncommon for people to realize that what they thought they needed isn't what they truly desire. At other times, the pendulum will help manifest exactly what people want. The best example would be Conrad Hilton, who carried a photograph of a prestigious hotel in his pocket. From time to time, he took out the picture and dowsed a pendulum to reinforce his desire to establish his own hotel. One day, his dream came true, and he became the owner of a global luxury hotel chain.

Chapter 2: Choosing Your Pendulum

Choosing your pendulum is the most important step of the process. The type of pendulum you select will depend on various factors. Many people are confused when choosing a pendulum for their spiritual and healing practices, which is understandable considering the extensive styles of pendulums available. Picking the right pendulum is crucial to the success of the process, whether you want to practice dowsing, grounding, or healing pendulum magic. So, while choosing your pendulum is a vital process, nothing stops it from being a fun experience.

Choosing your pendulum is the most important step of the process.
https://www.pexels.com/photo/woman-telling-fortune-with-silver-pendant-7391635/

While many people are curious about pendulum selection, there are no hard and fast rules that must be followed in this case. The choice depends on different factors, which will be discussed in this chapter. The final decision will ultimately come down to your preference.

When selecting your pendulum, it is essential to ensure that you're attracted to the pendulum and find it absorbing. This experience will differ for everyone, which is why there are no immutable rules surrounding this process. However, understanding the different types of pendulums and when they are most useful will come in handy when picking your pendulum. This chapter will introduce the numerous styles of pendulums available and explain what factors you should consider before selecting one. A pendulum selection checklist is also included at the end of the chapter.

If you're a beginner, one of the best pendulum styles uses a triangular or teardrop shape of a suitable material. What's great about these pendulums is that they don't weigh a lot and can easily be rotated. Plus, they won't cost you a fortune. That said, remember that this type of pendulum may not be suitable for you or compatible with the process you're going to practice. Bearing this in mind, it's critical that the pendulum you choose feels right for you and suits the purposes you have in mind.

Factors to Consider for Choosing a Pendulum

While there are countless factors you can consider when selecting a pendulum, the primary considerations should include the weight, shape, and material of the pendulum. These elements must be taken into account because they play a vital role in how the healing or other pendulum magic processes take place and their effectiveness.

1. Weight

Considering the pendulum's weight is of utmost importance when selecting one for any spiritual process. If you choose a heavy pendulum, you'll have to put in more effort during your practice. On the upside, heavy pendulums have the benefit of stronger feedback from these practices. The only downside is that you'll have to pay more attention to the pendulum. Otherwise, you risk losing control of it during practice.

By contrast, a lighter pendulum would be much easier to handle but will not provide the same level of connection as a heavier one. For example, suppose you're practicing dowsing with a light pendulum. In that case, you will not feel the same level of connection as you would with a heavy pendulum.

You can also try a medium-weighted pendulum, whose speed is neither too fast nor too slow, which gives the perfect response time compared to other pendulums. Their movement along the axis will also be just the right speed for a meaningful response.

2. Shape

Pendulums come in a plethora of shapes ranging from circular to angular ones. Others can be combination shapes merged together. Round pendulums are said to have a more feminine energy, whereas rectangular or square-shaped pendulums manifest more masculine energy. For example, a round dome ceiling seems more feminine when compared to the square top of a skyscraper. However, each of these shapes has a different vibe and cannot be completely classified as masculine or feminine.

The shape of a pendulum is a major consideration because the manifestation of energy produced by the pendulum depends on its structure. When selecting a shape, there's not much to remember except what feels genuinely attractive to your soul. Moreover, the pendulum's movement will also depend on what shape you select.

If you're selecting a pendulum specifically for the purpose of dowsing, opt for one that will move in imperfect circles during the process. To that end, try positioning the pendulum you're selecting the same way you would hold it while dowsing; then observe its path of motion. The pendulum doesn't necessarily have to be circular for this purpose, but it shouldn't be a shape that doesn't have a smooth, consistent rotation.

You'll witness that some of the commercially designed pendulums have a hollow compartment inside. These are called sample pendulums and are usually used to locate things. The hollow space is provided for you to put a sample of whatever it is you're searching for inside. For instance, if you're searching for water, put a small amount inside the pendulum's hollow portion. Similarly, insert oil if you're trying to locate oil using pendulum magic. Most basic shapes include drop-shaped, mermet-shaped, rectangular-shaped with hollow compartments, and crystal pendulums.

3. Material

A whole range of materials can be used to design the perfect pendulums for healing and spiritual practices. Usually, these pendulums are made of wood, brass, crystals, or other metals. Now, do you know which material works best for you? Since each type has specially defined purposes, when selecting your pendulum, keep a list of your requirements with you to find the most suitable one for your practice.

4. Brass

Brass pendulums are a superb choice when you need something durable. Although they will weigh more against other types of pendulums, their metallic nature inhibits any external energies from being absorbed into their structure. Therefore, these pendulums have neutral energy and don't need regular cleansing. Moreover, their movements are also suitable for different divination processes.

5. Stainless Steel

There are countless steel and stainless steel pendulums of various shapes. The best part about these pendulums is that they're made with different metals, including iron, nickel, chromium, silicon, and aluminum, which makes them more energy-conducive than their regular metal counterparts. Plus, many spiral-caged pendulums are designed to have a crystal placed within them. With that, you'll have the conductivity of both the metal and the crystal you decide to place. The best part is that it's very versatile. This way, you won't have to collect numerous crystal pendulums and can settle for a single steel pendulum and collect different crystals separately.

6. Wood

Wooden pendulums are usually designed to be bigger in size than their brass or crystal counterparts, but they're relatively lighter in weight. Like brass pendulums, wooden pendulums also have neutral energies and don't need to be cleansed as often as other materials. Wood is a durable material that will last longer if not exposed to water or other liquids. Plus, their response timing and position are superior to most pendulum materials.

7. Crystal

Many practitioners often prefer crystal pendulums due to their appealing structures and excellent response time. However, crystal pendulums tend to be more fragile in nature compared to brass or wood pendulum. So, if you drop it or slam it against something, cracks will likely form on the surface.

The best part about crystal pendulums is that they each manifest a different kind of energy. Crystal pendulums will have a distinctively unique energy signature, unlike other pendulum materials. For example, rose quartz is linked to the heart chakra and should be the crystal material of choice for relationship-related divination practices.

The specific attributes associated with the kind of crystal pendulum you select will determine the outcome of your practice. Many people even prefer to use their crystal pendulums as necklaces or charms and wear them as personal items. This is why selecting the one that matches your personality and doesn't hamper your natural energy is essential.

Unlike brass and wooden pendulums, crystal pendulums need to be cleansed to get rid of accumulated external energies. Crystal pendulums are so versatile that a whole chapter is dedicated to that topic later in the book. For a summary of the crystal types, you can consult the following table:

	Crystal	Association
1.	Agate	Balance, victory, protection
2.	Agate, Eye	Spiritual connection
3.	Agate, Moss	Relocation, new beginnings, job, house
4.	Amazonite	Creativity, communication, confidence
5.	Amber	Past

6.	Amethyst	Spiritual connection, psychic abilities, healing
7.	Aquamarine	Protection, peace, balanced emotions, elimination of fear
8.	Aventurine	Good fortune, good health, centering
9.	Beryl	Psychic awareness, creative opening, discovery
10.	Bloodstone	Prosperity, good health, protection from deceit and deception
11.	Carnelian	Protection from evil, confidence, and balancing
12.	Chalcedony	Aura cleansing, protection during travels
13.	Chrysocolla	Communication, protection, tension release
14.	Chrysoprase	Truth revelations, balancing
15.	Citrine	Prosperity, self-esteem, karmic lessons
16.	Fluorite	Grounding, healing, cleansing, past lives
17.	Hematite	Stress relief, grounding, courage
18.	Jade, blue	Relaxation, karmic influences

19.	Jade, green	Protection from evil, relaxation
20.	Jade, brown	Grounding, stabilizing
21.	Jasper, red	Protection from negative energies
22.	Jasper, green	Healing, balancing
23.	Jasper, brown	Grounding, stabilizing
24.	Labradorite	Spiritual connection
25.	Lapis lazuli	Psychic abilities, creativity, anxiety relief
26.	Malachite	Healing, evil repellent
27.	Obsidian, black	Eliminates negativity
28.	Obsidian, snowflake	Prosperity, protection, balancing
29.	Onyx, black	Destruction of negative energies
30.	Quartz, clear	Protection, spiritual connection
31.	Quartz, rose	Love, healing, balance
32.	Quartz, smoky	Grounding, centering, strengthening
33.	Tiger's eye	Insight, good luck, previous lives

| 34. | Tourmaline | Calming, clarity, success, good fortune, balance |
| 35. | Turquoise | Balance, communication, protection, psychic connection |

Selection of Pendulum Based on Its Use

Considering the primary goal of your pendulum, magic is essential before you can go about choosing one for the process. The material of the pendulum gives it unique properties that affect the final outcome of the divination or healing practice. This section will help you identify the optimal type of pendulum for your intended practice.

1. Healing

If the purpose of your pendulum magic is healing, balancing, or clearing spiritual blockages, you'll need to choose crystals that are linked to the chakras in question. Different crystals are associated with the seven chakras and are used to help them align, clear, or balance. You can also opt for copper or brass pendulums when planning to do an energy healing practice. The following table shows the seven chakras and the crystals associated with each of them:

	Chakras	**Associated crystals**
1.	Crown chakra	Clear quartz, moonstone, labradorite, amethyst
2.	Third eye chakra	Lapis lazuli, azurite
3.	Throat chakra	Turquoise, blue agate, aquamarine
4.	Heart chakra	Rose quartz, green agate, amazonite
5.	Solar plexus chakra	Citrine, amber, tiger's eye

6.	Sacral chakra	Carnelian, tiger's eye
7.	Root chakra	Black obsidian, tourmaline, bloodstone

2. Divination

If divination is your intended purpose, select a pendulum that can conduct higher spiritual energies and enhance your psychic abilities. It should also protect the wearer from any negative energies. You can refer to the list above to select a crystal suitable for this purpose. Usually, clear quartz pendulums are used for divination purposes. Not only can it conduct energy and transform it, but it also intensifies the energy, enhancing your abilities.

Another commonly used tool in divination includes the Merkaba pendulum. This type of pendulum helps connect with spiritual guides and establish universal connections. It is considered a multidimensional vessel that allows a link to be formed between different dimensions while also protecting the user. This type of pendulum also enables the brain to become more creative and solve problems.

Other crystals include Sheesham or Indian rosewood, which is connected to femininity. Associated with the heart chakra, this crystal pendulum is used to meditate when struggling with hindrances.

Using More Than One Pendulum

If you plan to practice dowsing, you can use multiple pendulums for this purpose. Instead of ordering a different pendulum for a certain purpose every time, get multiple pendulums and add them to your collection. You'll find that certain pendulums are more suited than others for specific tasks. This is why it's necessary to have a variety of crystals and other pendulums on hand. You can also use more than one pendulum together – try different combinations of crystals and see which ones work out best for you.

For beginners, a basic pendulum collection will typically include a teardrop-shaped pendulum, a triangular crystal pendulum, a conical beechwood pendulum, and a brass pendulum. That said, you're not strictly limited to these pendulums and can choose from the plethora of types available. Asking fellow enthusiasts or searching for recommendations online can help expand your horizons and allow you to make suitable acquisitions.

Bonus: Make Your Own Pendulum

While choosing a pendulum for divination and healing is a fun experience in itself, what's better than making your own pendulum from scratch? This can seem out of reach for beginners, but it really isn't. Crafting a pendulum at home is not as complicated as it sounds and takes just a few steps. Plus, this way, you'll have a deeper and more meaningful connection with your pendulum compared to a ready-bought one. You'll feel a sense of ownership of the pendulum and likely get a better response. You can make crystal and wooden pendulums with just a few basic supplies. Here's how to do it:

Crystal Pendulum

To craft a crystal pendulum, you'll need the following:

- Your preferred crystal or gemstone
- A thin wire or string
- A lightweight chain (metallic)
- Glue (optional)
- Sharp scissors

To make the pendulum:

1. Grab the wire and wrap it around the crystal until it forms a stronghold. Leave enough wire length at the end to form a loop. Alternatively, you can use glue to attach the crystal to the wire. Make sure you cut off any ends of the wire that are sticking out.

2. Bend the wire at the end to form a small loop. Connect one end of the chain on this loop and let the other end stay as it is. Make sure the length of the chain doesn't exceed 30cm or 12in.

3. To calibrate the pendulum, rest your elbow on a table, and hold the chain slightly above the table's surface. Decide which swing motions would be "yes," "no," or "unknown." For example, left to right motion can be yes, while up and down

motion can mean no, and a circular motion could mean unknown.

4. Keep the pendulum perfectly still, and ask a basic question you know the answer to. For example, you can ask, "Is the sky blue?" which you know is true.

5. Observe the pendulum's motion and see if it swings in the right direction. If not, try with another question or another material until you get an appropriate response.

Wooden Pendulum

To craft a wooden pendulum, you'll need the following:

- Thin, dry twigs
- Fine saw
- One small eye screw
- Woodburning tools
- Woodworking drill
- Sandpaper
- Waxed cotton cord

To make the pendulum:

1. You can use different kinds of wood to make this pendulum. Some people believe that different types of wood are used for certain purposes. So, use whatever type you deem appropriate. Make sure the twigs are dry and as straight as possible; this will help shape the pendulum. Try not to use freshly cut twigs, as they can break easily.

2. Firstly, remove the bark from the twigs using sandpaper. Make sure you use rougher sandpaper before moving on to finer ones. Keep scraping until the bark comes off completely and you get a smooth wooden surface. Also, straighten the twig when you're scraping off the bark.

3. Next, using sandpaper, you need to sharpen all four sides of the twig from one end. However, stop and check each side to ensure they're all even.

4. After you've created a tip, it's time to round it out by rubbing the twig on the sandpaper. Make a rolling movement with the twig over the sandpaper. However, make sure the tip becomes

perfectly round while also staying even. This step could take a while, but the end result will be worth it.

5. Once you're satisfied with how the tip of the pendulum looks, cut the desired length of the wood for your pendulum. You can use a fine saw for this purpose.

6. Now, work the sandpaper over the other end of the pendulum to get a round end on the other side. Make sure you get a smooth finish before moving on to decorating.

7. It's not necessary to decorate the pendulum. Still, it will certainly make it look better and bring you closer to your homemade magical tool. Using a woodburning tool, you can draw various patterns, symbols, and signs on the wooden pendulum.

8. Before drawing the permanent patterns on the pendulum, sketch out rough patterns using a pencil. Once you're satisfied with your drawings, it's time to make the final patterns using the woodburning tool. Make sure you don't apply too much pressure during this step.

9. Add in details, correct any mistakes, and take a final look at your work. You can also paint the wood using poster paints or use spray paint.

10. Now, drill a hole at the top of the pendulum (the rounded part) and attach the eye bolt. Make sure it is secure before inserting the chain or string through it. Use liquid glue if necessary.

11. Now, put the string through the loop, and add other small trinkets and decorations if desired.

Choosing a pendulum is the first step in pendulum magic, healing, and divination. As daunting as it can be for a beginner to select their first pendulum, it can be a fun and enriching experience. Selecting your pendulum requires great thought, care, and consideration. As you've seen, certain factors shouldn't be neglected when choosing your pendulums. Otherwise, the results of your readings could be disturbed. So, make sure your account for the pendulum's intended purpose before considering other important factors like weight, shape, and material. Understanding the various crystal types and how they can help with different spiritual and divination purposes is also important. In the end, don't overthink the process. If a pendulum calls out to you, you should definitely consider it for your practice, no matter the odds.

Chapter 3: Preparation and Cleansing

As you know by now, pendulums manifest energy not just on their own but also from their surrounding environment. This can be neutral, negative, or positive energy absorbed from various people and places before the pendulum gets to you. For instance, imagine that your pendulum was handmade with love by someone. It is likely to possess an abundance of positive energy. By contrast, if it was prepared or even simply packaged by someone going through difficult circumstances, the pendulum likely absorbed negative emotions and despairing energy.

A pendulum's energy should be cleansed and cleared like you cleanse your own aura.
https://www.pexels.com/photo/woman-meditating-with-pendulum-8770828/

This is why cleaning the pendulum before performing any divination is essential, even if you're using it for the first time. You never know where the pendulum had been before arriving at your doorstep. If you begin using it before any cleansing process, you'll likely get inaccurate and strange results or no results. A pendulum's energy should be cleansed and cleared in the same way you cleanse your own aura.

When you feel low, grumpy, or extremely pessimistic, it's clear that some negative forces are affecting your energy field. The same goes for divinatory tools, which need to be cleansed to eliminate any external energies to work perfectly. Fortunately, there are many ways you can do that. This chapter will go into detail about different cleansing techniques you can apply not just for your pendulums but for any other divinatory tools.

However, the single most important element of these techniques is your intention. The first step before any cleansing process is to set the intention for the practice. How do you do that? It's quite simple. First, you'll need to gather the materials you'll be using in the process. These could include salt, smudge sticks, water, soil, crystals, etc. Once you've done that, place the cleansing tool with your pendulum, close your eyes, and set the intention to remove unwanted energies from your pendulum with the help of the tools you're using.

Make sure you set the intention with kind words and thoughts instead of exhibiting stern behavior. If you set intentions in a bad mood, often, the purpose gets completed but not in an optimal way. So, it's better to avoid bad intentions. At last, you can start cleansing your pendulum in any of the ways described below:

1. Smoke

Smoke from smudge sticks has long been used to cleanse and clear energy. This tradition goes back to the Native Americans who used it to cleanse their auras. Usually, smudge sticks are made using sage, specifically white sage, but you can also use other herbs. These include rosemary, palo santo, lavender, eucalyptus, mugwort, sweetgrass, cedar, and any other herbs that boast cleansing properties.

How does smoke cleansing using herbs work? Basically, the negative ions of the smoke attach themselves to the positive ions floating around the aura of the tool that needs cleansing, which in this case, is a pendulum. Once these ions are removed, their energy is neutralized and stops affecting the performance of the pendulum. Because of this, the negative ions of the smoke take away the positive ions from the affected material and store this energy in the earth for transmutation.

To perform the cleansing process with smudge sticks, you must take the necessary safety precautions to ensure you don't end up hurting yourself or setting your house on fire. To do this, keep a heatproof bowl below the smudge stick while practicing the cleansing technique. This will ensure you catch any embers that fly out of the smudge stick. Once you light the smudge stick, don't blow it out instantly – let the flame die out by itself or shake it out. After this, you'll see a waft of smoke emanating from the stick. This is when you place the pendulum above the stick so that the smoke engulfs the pendulum. You'll know that the cleansing process has been successful by observing the color and movement of the smoke. If the smoke is thick and dark, there's a lot of energy left to clear, and when it becomes lighter, the energy has been cleared.

The movement of the smoke will also change once the pendulum has been cleansed. The smoke should move away from the pendulum once all negative energies have been evacuated. If you're in a room, make sure you open all the windows to let the smoke and negative energies leave the room. Once the process is done, leave the smudge stick in the heatproof bowl to burn out, or extinguish it with some sand.

2. Sunlight or Moonlight

One of the best and most effective ways to cleanse your pendulum of negative energy is through moonlight or sunlight. To cleanse under the moonlight, you'll have to do so on a full moon. This is because the full moon is the optimal time to release anything negative in your life. It is said that the moon is at its fullest power during the full moon and can pull all sorts of negative energies from the earth, just like it pulls the tides. So, if you want to cleanse your pendulum of negative energy, a full moon ritual is the perfect way to achieve that. To do this, you'll first need to set the intention of the ritual and then bring out your pendulum. Next, dip the pendulum into the purest water you can find, and make sure you do this under the moonlight. Once you're sure it's clean, remove it and dry it completely to prevent the metallic chain from rusting. Place the pendulum right under the moonlight, whether it's outside your house, on the roof, or simply on your windowsill. Retrieve the pendulum the next morning after dawn.

Alternatively, you can use sunlight as a technique to cleanse your pendulum of any negative energy. Sunlight is said to rejuvenate, recharge, and refresh objects. To perform this process, you must leave your pendulum in direct sunlight for a few hours. However, be mindful that this process is a bit harsher than moonlight rituals and should only last 3 to 4 hours. Some crystals like amethyst, rose quartz, citrine, and smoky quartz can fade if kept out in the sun for too long. Another thing you should be careful of is that some crystals in the quartz family can cause a fire when focusing on direct sunlight, so be mindful about where and how you place them.

3. Soil

Soil is one of the natural resources we can use to cleanse the negative energies of our divination tools. It not only helps grow, nourish, and ground energy but also clears any negative frequencies as well. To perform a soil cleansing, set the intention of clearing out negative energies from the pendulum and releasing them into the earth for transmutation. This process is said to be especially powerful for natural materials like crystal pendulums.

To perform the cleansing, place the pendulum in the soil of a potted plant or simply in open soil in your garden or yard. Leave it there for a few days until you feel that the negative energy has cleared away. Some people prefer to leave their pendulums in the dirt for a whole moon cycle to ensure all the negative entities have left the pendulum. When that is done, remove the pendulum from the dirt, and thank the earth for its favor.

4. Salt

Salt is considered an effective purifier and has been used to cleanse and clear away negative energies for centuries. Many people use it to ward off negative energy. Salt acts as a barrier to any negative or nasty energies, making it an ideal medium to cleanse your pendulum of inauspicious energy. You'll need a small bowl filled with sea salt or Himalayan salt to do this. Place the pendulum on top of the salt, or bury it underneath the mound of salt. Leave this overnight. Retrieve the pendulum the next morning with a cleansed, refreshed energy. Alternatively, you can mix salt with water and pour it over the pendulum to cleanse it. Another method of salt cleansing involves collecting seawater in a jar and using it to cleanse your pendulum's energy. However, if the chain of your pendulum is silver, salt cleansing is not a suitable method, as it can cause the chain to rust.

5. Water

Using water to purify and cleanse your pendulums is a great way to sift out all the negative energies that manifest themselves in them. Cleaning your pendulums with water isn't just good for when you need to cleanse them but also when other people have touched them. Since you don't want anyone else's energy on your pendulum, it's best to clean it right then and there. For the cleansing process, find the purest water you can find and run it over the pendulum. Suppose you have access to natural flowing springs or streams. In that case, that's even better because the water comes from Mother Nature herself. If not, use filtered or purified water for the best results.

In parallel, visualize white light while cleansing your pendulum with water, and imagine it flowing through the water over it. Unlike other cleansing techniques, you don't need to submerge the pendulum under water for long periods. Simply running water over the pendulum will suffice to restore balance to the pendulum's energies.

6. Light and Visualization

Visualization is an essential yet often underappreciated activity. In today's world, we only ever use the logical and analytical parts of the brain, often forgetting about the creative part. Using a visualization method to cleanse your pendulums will be fun and bring out your creative side. If you're not used to visualization, it's better to practice it first for a few days before you try this cleansing ritual on your pendulum.

You can do this by sitting outside in a calm atmosphere, closing your eyes, and imagining a white light descending from the sky and settling around you. Once you start feeling an energy shift, your process will be successful. The more you perform this exercise, the more easily the visualized light will come to you. You can also try to visualize other colors as well. Still, the most suitable color is white, as it symbolizes purity, peace, protection, and serenity. Other colors signify:

- **Yellow:** Intellect, strength, energy
- **Green:** Luck, fortune, prosperity, abundance, balance, healing
- **Orange:** Luck, confidence, success
- **Blue:** Safety, protection, tranquility, healing
- **Red:** Passion, desire, power, strength, vitality
- **Purple:** Wisdom, spiritual connection, protection
- **Pink:** Peace, emotional support, compassion, affection
- **Black:** Protection, binding, warding off negativity.

You can use a color that resonates with you or when you require the properties associated with it. You can also try to visualize a combination of these colors to design the perfect visual. For example, you should visualize the color purple when cleansing your pendulum and want to remove the stagnant energy. It will also improve your chances of connecting with the spiritual world while performing a divination technique. Similarly, you can visualize the color green when practicing healing rituals. Picture whichever shade of the color resonates best with your intuition and personal preference. The best part about visualization techniques is that there are no strict, set-in-stone rules. You only need to ensure your intentions are right, and the rest will go smoothly.

To perform visualization cleansing of your pendulum, sit in a quiet, comfortable place without distractions. Take a deep breath, hold it for a few seconds, and then exhale. Repeat this twice. Now, visualize white light surrounding you, towering all the way up to the sky. Visualize this light growing more intense and forming a large circle around you.

Now, visualize this light entering your body from your crown chakra and passing through each of the seven chakras, one by one. Finally, imagine this light flowing from your hands to the pendulum that you're holding. Imagine the light engulfing the pendulum and absorbing its negative energy. Then, visualize this light going out of the pendulum and into the ground, where it takes the negative energy to be dissipated. Once you get the hang of this process, cleaning your pendulums with white or any other colored light will only take a few minutes.

7. Crystals

Crystal cleansing is commonly used to dissipate or absorb negative energy from divination objects and tools. Using crystals to remove negative energies from crystal pendulums is the perfect example of using a diamond to cut another diamond. Thanks to the remarkable energy-clearing properties of certain crystals, this method is the most popular for cleansing pendulums. Some crystals that can be used for this process include:

- **Clear Quartz:** This highly effective crystal cleanser is one of the best options for a crystal cleansing ritual. You can keep a clear quartz crystal in the pouch you store the pendulum in – this will ensure that your pendulum stays free of any impure energies from its surroundings.

- **Selenite:** Considered a high vibrational crystal with exceptional cleansing powers, selenite is often used in crystal cleansing techniques. It has a positive energy field that helps protect any object, people, or space around it, freeing it from stagnant negative energy. However, ensure you do not place selenite in water, as it can dissolve very easily. Use a selenite rod to cleanse your pendulum by placing it on top of the crystal. Or, you can opt for a selenite wand and wave it around the pendulum to clear its energy field.

- **Black Obsidian:** A powerful crystal that can be used to remove any negative energy plaguing your pendulum. Add this crystal to your pendulum storage bag to protect the pendulum from inauspicious energies.

8. Sound

You'd be surprised to learn that sound cleansing techniques exist to clear away negative energies. Energies can be related to vibrations or frequencies; a sound is also a form of vibration. So, by using different sounds, the vibrations of negative energy can be dissipated from the pendulum. You can use sound tools like crystal bowls, drums, and singing bowls, but also singing, chanting – or even bells. To practice this technique, place the pendulum in a singing bowl and let the vibrations clear the negative energy. Alternatively, place the pendulum on a table and sound the cymbals three times. Make sure you open the windows to let the energy dissipate and avoid trapping it in the room.

Ultimately, the preparation and cleansing of crystals before using them for divination, dowsing, or healing and balancing practices is crucial to the success of the process. However, you can't always control what energies your pendulum absorbs. Both before it gets into your care and after you acquire it, you can effectively get rid of these energies so that these divination tools work properly. Remember that the most important element for cleansing or other processes involving pendulums is the intention set before the process. So, keep positive intentions, and the rest will work out well on its own. Now that you know how to properly cleanse your pendulum, it's time to take a closer look at how to program and charge it for your practice.

Chapter 4: Programming Your Pendulum

Once you've rid your pendulum of any negative energy thanks to cleansing, it's time to program it. Programming your pendulum is just as important as cleansing it. This step ensures that your tool is calibrated and ready to use. While you're probably wondering what the purpose of so many pre-ritual steps is and why you shouldn't jump into pendulum magic rituals directly, keep in mind that without these preliminary steps, you are most likely to get incorrect and off-the-charts readings. So, rather than skip these actions and come up empty-handed, it's best to be prepared. This chapter will provide a detailed guide to programming your pendulum, how to connect with it, and everything else you need to prepare before you can begin using it.

Programming your pendulum is just as important as cleansing it.
https://www.pexels.com/photo/woman-with-silver-pendulum-for-divination-7391631/

Creating a Sacred Space

Before you can program your pendulum, you'll first need to create a safe space for its use. Some people assume creating a safe space for pendulum magic means that negative or evil spirits will be involved, like in Ouija boards or seances. However, pendulum magic involves nothing of the sort. The need for a safe space arises because the space surrounding the pendulum must be cleared of any negative energy, just like the pendulum itself needs to be cleansed.

Understandably, not everyone will be able to designate a specific safe space for pendulum magic, in which case, any space will suffice as long as you cleanse the aura around it before the ritual. To create a safe space, find a small, comfortable spot in your house. This should be a place you're pulled towards and want to use creatively. Whether you designate this space in your bedroom, the lounge, or the study room *is up to you*. Gather things you believe connect to the rituals you plan to perform to add a familiar touch to this space. These can include crystals, wands, shells, figurines, candles, or anything that brings you closer to your pendulum.

Your pendulum kit can also be arranged somewhere in the designated sacred space. Whether you decide to place these items on the floor, a table, a cabinet, or anywhere else is your choice. While decorating this space, let your creative side guide you into finding new ways to decorate the space. Make use of a rug, some fabrics, cushions, and lace cloths to personalize the space. The space doesn't have to be circular in nature or of any general shape.

Most people use their pendulums on a table and sometimes on the floor in front of an altar they've created. Once you've finished decorating the space, take a position at the table or on a cushion on the floor, and observe the energy around the room. If you feel that the room's energy needs cleansing, you can use one of the methods discussed in the previous chapter to shift this energy. For example, if you want to clear the room's energy with smoke, make sure you keep the windows open to let the negative energy go out.

The surrounding energy fields during a pendulum ritual must be completely neutral, free-flowing, and natural. This ensures that any negative energies don't interact with your pendulum and prompt incorrect readings. Before any pendulum reading, you can try the white light visualization activity to further charge this space. To do this, place yourself within the sacred space, sitting or standing, straighten your spine, and close your eyes. Now, visualize a white light surrounding you, growing brighter and stronger until it finally engulfs you and the sacred space, forming a halo of protection around the space.

Then, you can meditate for a few moments before you move on to programming your pendulum for the ritual. To do this, close your eyes and take a few deep breaths. Focus on your breathing, and try to center your brain. Now, direct your intentions for the ritual towards the pendulum. Before meditating, you can light candles or use herbal incense to appease the atmosphere and raise your energy.

Programming Your Pendulum

Once you've created a safe, sacred space, it's time to start programming your pendulum. First, hold the top of the pendulum using your dominant hand's thumb and index finger. There should be a bead or some other small item at the top of the pendulum to hold it. Now, place your elbow on the table, or, if you're sitting on the floor, rest your elbow on your thigh or keep it still and steady. Make sure your wrist stays straight while your elbow remains slightly bent. Your arm should look straight and aligned.

Hold the pendulum with a relaxed grip to ensure there are no restrictions to its movements. Once in a stable, comfortable position, you're now ready to program the pendulum. To do this, you must ensure that the pendulum swings as it is supposed to for yes/no/maybe answers. Although there are no strict rules to follow regarding the pendulum's movement, and the readings depend on your intention and skill, most people prefer to consider the backward and forward movement of the pendulum as "yes." For "no" answers, the pendulum should move sideways or left to right. If the answer to the question is "maybe," the pendulum will move counterclockwise. For a "not now" response, the pendulum will most likely not move, which indicates that now is not the time for this question to be answered. In that case, the procedure should be repeated some other time.

However, these movements aren't the same for every pendulum and every person. This is why programming each pendulum before the ritual is so essential – ensuring its movements align with your considerations and that you do not end up giving wrong readings. The beauty of using a pendulum is that obtaining accurate readings will no longer seem difficult or impossible once you get the hang of its movements. So, before starting any pendulum magic, you must program your pendulum to align with these movements for optimal results.

Connecting with Your Pendulum

Invariably, you'll have to show some patience and get through some important steps before you can start swinging your pendulum and finding answers. Connecting with your pendulum is crucial if you want to get accurate readings, that is, with minimum errors. You must familiarize yourself with how the pendulum swings by practicing, trusting, and focusing on the pendulum. If you pick up the pendulum and start asking questions straight away, you'll get no response, or worse, a completely opposite response to the truth.

So, it's important to keep practicing and getting familiar with the nature of the pendulum. Ideally, you should give your pendulum one week in which you practice using it daily to understand its rhythm and movement. Unlike other divination techniques, you can't simply pick up a card and start interpreting the readings. Pendulum magic requires weeks and months of practice, and when you finally master it, only then will you start getting accurate results. Gradually ease your way into the swinging process of the pendulum, and while focusing on the pendulum, trust yourself, letting go of any expectations, urgency, or intrusive thoughts. Simply let your brain blank out by only focusing on the swing of the pendulum, and let the rest of the process happen naturally.

Aim to set aside fifteen minutes every day during the first week after you program your pendulum to form a connection with it. During this time, sit in your sacred space and simply spend time around your pendulum. You can either meditate, try some yoga, or practice visualization exercises to help establish a connection. This step will prove to be a wonderful experience in your pendulum magic journey while also giving you time to unwind, relax and meditate.

Getting to Know Your Pendulum Exercise

Start this exercise by cleansing yourself, your environment, and your pendulum. You can do this by employing any of the techniques mentioned in the previous chapter. Once you're confident that all negative energies have been cleared away and you feel uplifted and in good spirits, get into a comfortable position within the sacred space. First, you'll need to dissociate from the rest of the world and any problems in your life. Meditation is the best way to achieve this. Practice a meditative sequence that can relax you and help you focus.

You can also decide to use crystals and other spiritual tools during your meditative session. During meditation, concentrate on your breathing and let any other thought leave your mind. Once your mind has cleared and you're in a state of tranquility, take hold of your pendulum and begin to program it. Once you've finished programming it, as explained above, start asking basic questions with yes/no/maybe answers. It is better to ask questions you know the answers to at this early stage instead of queries you're unsure of.

Once you get the hang of how it moves, how long it takes to swing, and if it answers the question correctly, this will help you get to know your pendulum better. During your questioning session, you'll observe that vague questions result in little to no movement of the pendulum, whereas clear questions have an instantaneous response. With that in mind, you must confidently voice your questions using clear, precise wordings. Pendulums swing differently for everyone, so don't despair if your pendulum only swings gently while you've seen others swing great distances.

With time and practice, your pendulum will start to swing as you expect it to. Once you feel enough time has passed and you've started to bond with it, allow the pendulum to move more freely and relax.

Signs That Your Pendulum Works Correctly

The movement of your pendulum depends primarily on your consciousness or subconsciousness. The phrase "Intention is everything" should be considered because it holds true value. While many people consider there to be a universal guide that dictates the movement of pendulums, your subconscious energy actually guides the whole process. For example, suppose you ask your pendulum a question about whether you'll win the lottery. In that case, you're more likely to get an affirmative answer because, subconsciously, that is what you want. The pendulum's clockwise, anticlockwise, sideways, and forward/backward movements are programmed in the same way. You'll cause the pendulum to move in certain directions, and it will, through the invisible energy of your aura.

Once you're properly connected with the pendulum, it will move in the way you tell it to. However, why use it to ask divination questions at all if this is the case? In fact, while pendulums' movement depends on your subconscious energy, once you neutralize your energy, the movement will not be dictated by your desires. Despite that, it can be rather difficult to remain neutral on many topics. For instance, if you ask a question that has emotional significance to you, you'll likely get a biased response from the pendulum due to your energy imbalance. This is why you're advised to meditate and then ask questions calmly and neutrally. Because of this, asking clear questions with simple yes/no answers is best in these readings.

If there's a complex problem you need help with, the best approach is to divide the problem into simpler, yes/no/maybe answer questions and then address them. Once you achieve neutrality and detach yourself from the problem, you're more likely to get an accurate response. Another way you can get viable responses from your pendulum is by using pendulum charts, which will be discussed in detail in an upcoming chapter. These charts will make it easier for you to find answers to your questions.

Storing Your Pendulum

Storing your divination tools is important and should be carried out with great care. Once you've cleansed and programmed your pendulum, you need to store it safely. You'll also need to ensure the crystals on your pendulums are not damaged when kept together. With that in mind, keeping any rough crystals away from tumbled stones is best. Make sure you store them in such a way that they don't scratch each other. If stored carelessly, the surface and luster of the crystal pendulums will be damaged, which may affect the pendulum's movement and overall effectiveness.

If you have a spare jewelry box, you can store each pendulum in a separate compartment of the box. Better yet, you can create a DIY pendulum box. All you need is a box with some compartments; if there are no compartments, you can always add some with a few creative crafts. Another option is to hang them like you would hang necklaces. A necklace holder will make the perfect place to hang your pendulums and keep them in your sacred space.

You should also be careful of your crystal pendulums' chemical and physical compatibility. For example, crystals like selenite and rose quartz are soft in nature and can be easily scratched. Some crystals are also sensitive to water or moisture exposure and will disintegrate if scratched. So, keeping these crystal pendulums safe from moisture and other abrasive materials is crucial. For this purpose, you can wrap them in a soft cloth and store them safely.

Storing each separately for bigger crystal pendulums is essential to ensure they don't damage other crystals. Smaller stones and crystals can be stored in a silk or satin pouch. In order to keep your pendulums pure and effective, always treat them with care and responsibility. When traveling with your pendulums, wrap each one in a separate silk cloth to avoid abrasion. If you don't have access to silk cloths, you can always use eyeglass cloths or even tissue paper to wrap your crystals. Here are other things you should keep in mind:

- Certain crystal types can get faded when kept under direct sunlight. These include citrine, opal, fluorite, aquamarine, topaz, and others. Make sure you practice moon cleansing for these crystal pendulums and store them away from sunlight.

- If you do end up damaging your crystal pendulum, you may still be able to salvage it. If only the surface has been chipped, try to cleanse and program it again. If it shows correct responses, then it's fine. Otherwise, you'll have to replace it.

While pendulum magic is not as complicated as one may imagine it to be, it does have its share of processes and learning. Each process holds a level of importance that cannot be neglected. So, instead of finding shortcuts, it's better to acknowledge the significance of each step and practice them until you perfect them. Programming your pendulum is not something that should be taken lightly. An incorrectly programmed pendulum is as good as a broken one. Make sure to follow and refer back to the guidelines provided in this chapter to have a fully functioning, reliable pendulum.

Chapter 5: Pendulums and Crystals

The popularity of crystals has been growing in the last few years. Something mysterious about their shapes and alluring colors just captures the imagination. However, this isn't the main reason behind their popularity. Crystal healing has become a popular alternative medicine; hence more and more people are curious about these pretty stones. The use of crystals isn't something new. In fact, people have been using crystals throughout history, whether as accessories, home decorations, or to benefit from their healing powers. Nowadays, people still use crystals for the same reasons.

In essence, crystals are minerals that are usually created underground. Each crystal is unique, not just in its shape and color but in its healing properties. Some crystals have peculiar shapes – some are very small, whereas others can be quite large. Crystals can form under various conditions, impacting their shape and color. They come from nature, where they get their energies from the ocean, the moon, or the sun.

Due to their chemical structures, crystals can store energy. Similar to how your brain works, it stays in your memory once you see something. Once a crystal experiences a type of energy, it can carry it forever or until you cleanse it. When you program a crystal by holding it and setting an intention, it will remember and spread this type of energy wherever you place it. For instance, if you set an intention of peace while holding a crystal and place it in your home, it will make your environment more peaceful. Crystals have the power to hold all types of energies, even negative ones, which is why they require cleansing after being exposed to inauspicious energies.

As it happens, crystals don't just spread positive energy around your home. You can place crystals on certain areas of your body to take advantage of their physical, psychological, and emotional benefits. Crystals emit certain vibrations that can interact with your body's energetic frequency – this interaction can create balance in the body to make you feel relaxed and focused. This insightful chapter will delve into the fascinating world of crystals and how you can use them in your pendulum practice.

Crystals and Pendulum Practices

Crystals play a significant role in numerous pendulum practices. You can use their healing abilities against physical ailments to restore your energy or even reconnect with the earth.

Physical and Energy Healing

Crystals can provide healing and protection against various diseases. They act as channels that allow positive and healing energy to flow through your body, pushing out the negative energy causing your ailment. Crystals boast healing properties, and different crystals can help with specific diseases. For example, green aventurine can remedy heart issues. Celestite can alleviate sleeping problems, and amethyst can help people suffering from intestine issues. When someone suffers from a physical condition, the healer should first identify the root cause so they can choose the appropriate crystal to treat their ailment.

Balancing Chakras

As you've seen, your body has seven main energy centers called *chakras*. These centers are responsible for supplying subtle energy to different organs. Each chakra corresponds to one or more of your major organs and nerve bundles and greatly impacts your mental, emotional, spiritual, and physical health. When your chakras are balanced or opened, they allow for the flow of energy throughout your body, keeping you healthy and energetic. However, if any of your chakras are blocked or unbalanced, you'll likely feel your physical and mental health are suffering. Keeping your chakras open is vital to your well-being; this is where crystals come in.

Using crystals is one of the most effective ways to unblock your chakras. Each crystal has unique properties that can connect with the body's energy field and tune into your chakras to restore their balance. Since crystals emit different vibrations, you must use a crystal that has vibrations that target the chakra that requires balancing. There are several crystals associated with each of the seven chakras. Using the right crystal for the blocked chakra will guarantee that the healing process takes place effectively.

The Root Chakra

The root chakra, or Muladhara, is located at the base of the spine. It is responsible for making you feel secure and safe. When this chakra is out of balance, you may suffer from hip or lower back issues and experience anxiety and depression. The best crystals for balancing the root chakra should be dark and have protective and grounding properties. This chakra is also associated with the colors red, silver, brown, and black, so opt for crystals of those colors, including:

- Black Tourmaline
- Obsidian
- Smoke Quartz
- Bloodstone
- Red Jasper
- Mystical Merlinite

The Sacral Chakra

The sacral chakra, or Swadhisthana, is located in the lower abdomen. It is associated with sexuality and creativity. When this chakra is out of balance, you may experience issues with your libido and struggle with sexual expression and pleasure. The best crystals to use for this chakra are orange since this color is most associated with the sacral chakra. Some include:

- Carnelian
- Orange calcite
- Orange jasper

- Sunstone

- Peach moonstone

Solar Plexus Chakra

The solar plexus chakra, or Manipura, is located around the navel area. This chakra is responsible for your willpower and self-worth. You may become angry, controlling, and powerless when it's unbalanced. You may also experience physical symptoms like indigestion. Yellow and gold crystals are ideal for bringing balance to the solar plexus chakra and can include the following:

- Yellow jasper

- Tiger's eye

- Citrine

- Pyrite

The Heart Chakra

The heart chakra, or Anahata, is located in the center of the chest. Unsurprisingly, this energy center is responsible for all matters related to romance, compassion, and empathy. When this chakra is out of balance, you may not be able to feel empathy or connect with others and may struggle with letting go of grudges. Green but also pink crystals will open up your blocked heart chakra. These include:

- Rhodochrosite

- Rose Quartz

- Malachite

- Jade

- Emerald

- Jade

- Peach Moonstone

The Throat Chakra

The throat chakra, or Vishuddha, is located in the throat area. It is responsible for communication, speaking, and self-expression. When this chakra is unbalanced, you may lie and gossip, feel confused, and be left unable to express yourself. Blue crystals are your best option for bringing balance to the throat chakra, including:

- Blue Kyanite
- Blue Apatite
- Lapis Lazuli
- Amazonite
- Sodalite
- Aquamarine

Third Eye Chakra

The third eye chakra, or Ajna, is located right between the eyebrows. It is responsible for dreams and imagination. When this chakra is out of balance, you may feel that your thoughts are out of control and experience brain fog and delusions. Indigo and violet crystals will help with unblocking the third eye chakra. These include:

- Lepidolite
- Lapis lazuli
- Amethyst
- Labradorite

The Crown Chakra

The crown chakra, or Sahasrara, is the last of the seven chakras. Located at the top of the head, this chakra is responsible for connecting you with the universe and finding your purpose. When unbalanced, you may not be enthusiastic about your future and lose your sense of purpose. When it comes to unblocking the crown chakra, stick to white and violet crystals, such as:

- Moonstone
- Selenite
- Celestite
- Crystal Quartz
- Golden Heart

Grounding

Another pendulum practice where crystals can be effective is grounding. Grounding allows you to connect with the energy of the earth. It enables you to be calm, collected, centered, and balanced, especially during times of turmoil. Feeling grounded is associated with being true to yourself and clear thinking to make good life decisions. If you feel that you're losing your connection with the earth and life has made you unsettled, crystals can ground you and help you rekindle your balance. They will allow you to connect with the earth's energy, wisdom, and everything it offers.

There are specific crystals that are powerful enough to bring stability and strength back into your life. These will help you live in the present moment without worrying over the past or concerning yourself with the future. They can also help you let go of any negative energy affecting your spirit, body, and mind. Grounding crystals can also provide protection and prevent toxic energy from disturbing your inner peace. This section will go over some of the most effective crystals for grounding.

Hematite

Hematite is a powerful crystal that can ground you and reconnect you with the earth. It will restore your balance while releasing negative emotions like anxiety and insecurity. Hematite can also rebalance your root chakra, which is responsible for your sense of stability. That way, you'll allow the energy to flow through your body to make you feel grounded.

Hematite can rebalance your root chakra.

As mentioned, many grounding crystals also provide protection, and hematite is one of them. It will protect you against negative energy threatening your stability and balance. This dynamic crystal acts like a magnet that pulls you down to earth.

Smoky Quartz

Another powerful grounding crystal is smoky quartz. It can rid you of negative emotions like restlessness, stress, and fear. Once these emotions are released, you'll experience feelings of clarity, calmness, and grounding. Smoky quartz replaces emotions that don't serve you with positive ones that will benefit your spirit, mind, and body. For instance, if you are prone to anxiety, this crystal can help you put these feelings into perspective and work through them instead of letting them disturb your peace.

Smoky quartz replaces emotions that don't serve you with positive ones.
Ra'ike (see also: de:Benutzer:Ra'ike), CC BY-SA 3.0
<https://creativecommons.org/licenses/by-sa/3.0>, via Wikimedia Commons:
https://commons.wikimedia.org/wiki/File:Quartz_-_Smoky_quartz_from_Obersulzbachtal_-_Austria.jpg

Smoky quartz can be a better option for some people compared to hematite. Hematite's energy is so powerful that it can feel overwhelming, which is typically not the case for smoky quartz, thanks to its more subtle kind of energy.

Black Tourmaline

Black Tourmaline is associated with the root chakra.
https://pixabay.com/es/photos/turmalina-negra-muestra-roca-rock-1609432/

Black tourmaline acts as a protective stone against negative energy. It is also associated with the root chakra, which, when balanced, can provide grounding and stability. This crystal can also boost your confidence, increase your strength, and make you feel steady. Black tourmaline can connect you with nature so you can feel safe and secure, releasing feelings like anxiety and fear in the process.

Jasper

It isn't uncommon for a person to lose their way in life. Luckily, jasper can help you reconnect with the Earth and find your way back to yourself, especially during times of uncertainty. This crystal can bring you balance and stability while providing you with determination, strength, and courage. When you feel exhausted or overwhelmed in your everyday life, the jasper crystal can reenergize you and refresh your body and mind. It can also bolster your creativity whenever you feel stuck or uninspired.

Jasper can help you reconnect with the Earth.
https://pixabay.com/es/photos/piedras-rocas-jaspe-jaspe-rojo-7182407/

People have been using jasper for centuries for its grounding and healing properties. This crystal contains powerful earth energy that can strengthen your bond with the earth. While there are several types of jasper stones with different shades, they all have strong earth energy inside of them.

Obsidian

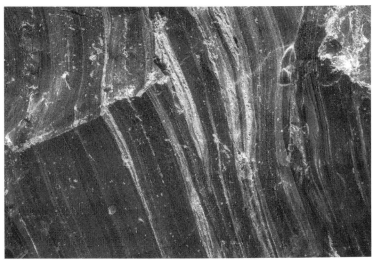
Obsidian acts as a shield to protect you against negative emotions.
https://www.pexels.com/photo/close-up-of-obsidian-4766367/

Obsidian has remarkable grounding properties that can balance and stabilize your spirit, mind, and body. It isn't rare for people to suppress certain negative emotions, which can directly impact their mental and physical health. Obsidian can help you become aware of these feelings so you can confront them instead of running away from them. It also acts as a shield to protect you against negative emotions.

Onyx

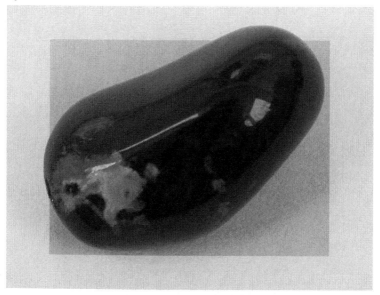

Onyx provides guidance and reassurance whenever you feel afraid or unsure about your future.
Simon Eugster --Simon 14:41, 11 April 2006 (UTC), CC BY-SA 3.0 <http://creativecommons.org/licenses/by-sa/3.0/>, via Wikimedia Commons: https://commons.wikimedia.org/wiki/File:Onyx.jpg

Not only is onyx a grounding stone, but it can also release stress and bring balance and harmony back into your life. Whenever you experience fear, onyx has the power to support you until you can get rid of these feelings for good. Various negative emotions often accompany anxiety, worry, and stress. This crystal can eliminate these feelings and replace them with positive ones. If you ever feel out of your comfort zone, onyx can help you through these situations. This crystal will also provide guidance and reassurance whenever you feel afraid or unsure about your future. The onyx crystal is associated with several chakras: the third eye chakra, the root chakra, the crown chakra, and the solar plexus chakra.

Types of Crystal Pendulums

Chakras Healing Pendulums

The first type of crystal pendulum is the chakra healing pendulum. A crystal pendulum can unblock your chakras to improve your emotional, spiritual, mental, and physical health. By using this method, you'll be able to determine the energy level in each chakra to see which ones require balancing, so you can begin the healing process. The best tool for this method is the seven-chakra pendulum, as it features all the main crystals of the seven chakras:

- Amethyst
- Red jasper
- Iolite
- Carnelian
- Lapis lazuli
- Green aventurine
- Golden calcite

You can use this type of pendulum to communicate with your higher self and spirit guides and ask them any questions on your mind. This pendulum is ideal for people working with chakras and looking to bring balance to any or all of the seven chakras.

Divination Pendulums

Various crystals can be used for divination purposes. This type of pendulum can raise your higher spiritual energy and protect you from negative vibes. Crystals known to intensify and transform your energy include quartz of various shades.

Healing Crystals

As established, crystals have strong healing properties. If you plan to start working with crystal pendulums, it's good to be aware of the most common crystals and learn about how they can help you. These include:

Angelite

Angelite can provide guidance and help you work with your higher self.
Didier Descouens, CC BY-SA 3.0 <https://creativecommons.org/licenses/by-sa/3.0>, via
Wikimedia Commons: https://commons.wikimedia.org/wiki/File:Anhydrite_Arnave.jpg

Angelite is one of the most popularly used crystals in pendulums. It is suitable for divination and spiritual work, as it can help you connect with your spiritual guides. This light blue crystal can also provide guidance and help you work with your higher self.

Rose Quartz

Rose Quartz can help restore balance to the heart chakra.
https://www.pexels.com/photo/rose-quartz-crystals-on-glass-surface-4391421/

Rose quartz is a favorite among many people, especially those who seek healing for matters of the heart. This crystal can help restore balance to the heart chakra. The rose quartz is ideal for people struggling with forgiveness, as it can help them let go of the past so they can forgive others and, most of all, forgive themselves. It can also help you love and accept yourself for who you are and happily receive love from others. This crystal emits vibrations of unconditional love and heals the body, mind, and spirit by bringing you harmony and balance.

Clear Quartz

Clear quartz can provide clarity to the mind.
https://www.pexels.com/photo/a-cluster-of-quartz-crystal-9037438/

Clear quartz is perhaps the most popular healing crystal, and for a good reason. It is often referred to as "the master healer." Clear quartz can bring balance to any of your seven chakras and provide clarity to the mind. It can also attune to the energies of any other crystal. Another advantage to this crystal is that you can easily program it to access a higher state of consciousness. You can also use this crystal in various rituals, including grounding and self-healing.

Kunzite

Kunzite will provide you with an abundance of love and compassion.

No one can live without love and compassion. If you find your life lacking these two emotions, give kunzite a chance. It will provide you with an abundance of love and compassion. This crystal has various healing properties, helping you heal from past relationships, cleanse your aura, and open your heart to the love and acceptance of those around you. Thanks to its grounding and calming properties, kunzite can also help bring harmony into your life.

Citrine

Citrine can help you release negative energy and replace it with positivity.
https://pixabay.com/es/photos/citrino-gemas-cristal-brillante-7433765/

Everyone needs a little sunshine and positivity in their lives. This yellow, sun-shaded crystal can impart positive vibrations into your life, making you grateful and more appreciative of everything you have. Citrine can help you release negative energy and replace it with positivity. It promotes growth and pushes you to achieve your goals with a positive attitude. This crystal is associated with the solar plexus chakra and can restore its balance.

Malachite

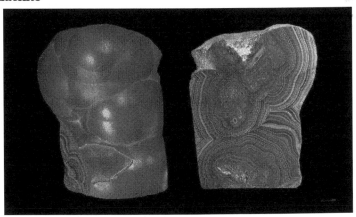

Malachite can offer deep healing, protection, and energetic support.
Didier Descouens, CC BY-SA 3.0 <https://creativecommons.org/licenses/by-sa/3.0>, via Wikimedia Commons: https://commons.wikimedia.org/wiki/File:Malachite_Kolwezi_Katanga_Congo.jpg

Malachite is the crystal of bravery, providing you with courage and strength. Suppose your life abounds with uncertainty and fear, especially regarding money. In that case, this crystal can offer deep healing, protection, and energetic support. Whatever pain, wounds, or old trauma you have experienced in your life, malachite will help you overcome these emotions and move on from loss and heartache.

Moonstone

Moonstone can enrich your life with positive feelings.

Moonstone has several healing properties. It can help you remain focused, provides support, and helps you balance your emotions. It can also help you establish a deep connection with the divine feminine. Moonstone can enrich your life with positive feelings like acceptance, curiosity, patience, acceptance, and nurturing.

Lepidolite

Lepidolite can provide a sense of calmness to your nervous system.
© Zbynek Burival / Mineralexpert.org:
https://commons.wikimedia.org/wiki/File:Lepidolite_from_Rozna_Czech_Republic.jpg

Lepidolite calms and relaxes the body and mind. If your emotions are boiling, your body is tense, and your mind is stressed, this crystal can help soothe all these intense feelings. Lepidolite can provide a sense of calmness to your nervous system and help people suffering from anxiety, insomnia, or panic disorder.

Black Tourmaline

Black tourmaline can help release underlying negative emotions.
Texas Lane, CC BY-SA 4.0 <https://creativecommons.org/licenses/by-sa/4.0>, via Wikimedia Commons: https://commons.wikimedia.org/wiki/File:Raw_Black_Tourmaline.jpg

When negative energy flows through your body, it affects your well-being and consumes you, and leaves no room for positivity. Black tourmaline can help release underlying negative emotions and free up space for positive energy. This crystal also acts as a powerful protective stone that can shield you from external negative energy.

Amethyst

Amethyst has physical, emotional, and spiritual healing properties.
https://www.pexels.com/photo/set-of-shiny-transparent-amethysts-grown-together-4040567/

Derived from the Greek "amethystos," the word amethyst means "not intoxicated." The ancient Greeks believed this crystal to hold protective powers that could protect people from the effects of intoxication from alcohol. In fact, the ancient Egyptians, Romans, and Greeks all harnessed the healing powers of this crystal. It has a characteristic glassy luster and comes in eye-catching shades of purple and violet. Amethyst is considered a bridge that connects the physical and the divine world. It has always been associated with spirituality and spiritual healing and is known to bring back balance to the crown chakra and third eye chakra. Amethyst has physical, emotional, and spiritual healing properties. It can keep you calm, help you to make better decisions, balance your emotions, give you courage, boost your immune system, heal migraines, and reduce negative energy.

Selenite

Selenite can heal the body and mind.

Selenite is associated with consciousness and clarity, and people often refer to it as the "goddess stone." Selenite is derived from Selene, the Greek goddess of the moon, who was a powerful deity that could bring light to the darkest of nights. Thanks to its name and association with the Greek goddess, Selenite is considered one of the most spiritual crystals in the world. Its color is often compared to angel wings, which adds to its mysticism. It is known for its soothing properties and can bring harmony and protection. Selenite can heal the body and mind, helping to realign the skeleton, manage anxiety, and bring balance to the heart chakra.

How to Choose a Crystal Pendulum

One of the first things people do before choosing a crystal is checked out its description. However, this information isn't always comprehensive or helpful. Each person will have a unique experience with the crystals they use. The information you read only shows one aspect of what the crystals offer. This doesn't mean you should ignore this information, as it can give you an idea of what each crystal can do. Don't rely on it completely when making a decision.

Do you choose a crystal, or does the crystal choose you? Select the crystals that speak to you and those you feel most drawn to or connected with. While choosing a crystal purely based on shape and color is tempting, you're looking for something much deeper and more personal. Hold different crystals in your hand and try to identify what you are feeling. Pick the crystal that you experience an energetic connection with.

To narrow down your options and better understand what to look for, identify your issues so you can select the stone with the appropriate healing properties. Make sure you follow your intuition and look for a connection.

Crystals have been around for thousands of years, and many people have used them for their numerous beneficial properties. Today, people wear crystals or place them around their homes to reap their natural benefits. Crystals have become a part of various pendulum practices, as they provide healing properties and can bring balance to the seven chakras. Whether it's divination, balancing chakras, or grounding, you can always count on crystals to satisfy your spiritual needs.

Chapter 6: Pendulums for Dowsing and Divination

This chapter discusses what it takes to develop your skills for pendulum dowsing and divination. Before that, you'll learn what divination is and what it isn't. You'll get to delve much deeper into these two terms, laying the foundation for a successful practice. Last, but not least, you'll discover how intuition is linked to divination – something you'll read more about later in the book.

Pendulum dowsing is one of the earliest recorded methods of divination.
https://pixabay.com/es/photos/p%c3%a9ndulo-la-radiestesia-espiritual-4868645/

What Is Divination?

Divination can be defined in many ways, with the most common description being the art of predicting the future. However, while divination methods can reveal certain aspects of the future, they're not fortune-telling. No divination method will provide precise answers about your future because you're constantly shaping it with your behavior. Even the smallest thought can lead to behavior that changes the course of your life and affect the future. For that reason, divination should only be viewed as a tool to gain insight into events, situations, or questions about a person's life. This insight is the potential outcome of the behavior dictated by the thoughts in your subconscious mind. Divinatory tools help tap into these thoughts and access information that otherwise wouldn't be accessible. The subconscious part of your mind stores this information as ingrained thought patterns. Divinatory tools can help you translate these into images or other stimuli that you can perceive with the conscious part of your mind. Apart from your subconscious mind, the information can also come from other higher beings, such as ancestral souls and spiritual guides.

Several forms of divination include dream interpretation, tarot card divination, runecasting, reading tea leaves, scrying, crystal ball divination, pendulum dowsing, and other techniques. As with any other method, pendulum dowsing requires you to learn how to interpret messages – which is only possible if you're able to tap into your intuition. After all, you're gaining a higher knowledge only your higher self can decipher. The best way to reach your higher self is by tapping into your gut. Why? Because dowsing (and divination itself) is a form of communication in which you rely on energy. You're connecting your intuitive power with the life forms around you, so you can interpret the messages you receive. Whether you seek knowledge and assistance from your spiritual guides or simply want to communicate with them, you'll need your intuition to get the message through.

Divination is an ancient form of predicting the future, and pendulum dowsing is one of the earliest recorded methods. Its simplicity makes it the ideal tool for beginners, as pendulums are easy to make, use, and maintain between sessions. As explained earlier, the questions posed during pendulum divinatory dowsing practices are also straightforward, with simple "yes" or "no" answers. As long as the questions are specific enough, you can find plenty of information in these simple answers. That said, dowsing only entails confirming the information you already have in your subconscious. You're not foreseeing new facts. There are several ways to apply this to divination, and you can tailor the methods to your liking.

Now, before embarking on your dowsing journey, you'll need to decide the reasons for starting it. Despite popular belief, simply wanting to know your future isn't a good enough cause. For your reason to be compelling, it needs to be realistic and formulated in a way that helps you grow. Remember, you're the creator of your own reality. You're the only one who knows how to shape your future the way you want it to look. You can manifest a future outcome, but you'll also be able to work for it. So, after receiving a message about a future event, you'll need to analyze it and see what you can do to make it come to life. Divination is one of the purest and most accurate forms of understanding the future. That said, it takes serious and consistent practice until you master this art.

Pendulum Dowsing in Detail

First and foremost, you must consider your pendulum as an extension of your intuitive energy. The type of tools you use for dowsing always depends on what feels right for you at the moment. Whether you buy a pendulum or create one on your own, it only matters that you can connect it to your intuition – and yes, your gut will let you know whether you have the right tool. Crystals are the most common choice for pendulum dowsing. Some popular crystals used for dowsing include:

- **Amethyst:** Often associated with the spiritual world.
- **Clear Quartz:** Linked to mental clarity and the connection to a higher purpose.
- **Rose Quartz:** Popular for grounding and calming the senses before dowsing rituals.

Since different occasions may require different energies, you can have several pendulums for dowsing. For beginners, choosing only one pendulum and practicing your dowsing and divination skills with it is recommended. Once you get the hang of interpreting simple messages, you'll be able to upgrade to more complex practices.

Before you start using your pendulum, you should always prepare it (cleansing and charging it with your energy, as described in the previous chapters). This is a crucial step for making it work with your intuition. Whichever method you choose to ensure the tools are enveloped only in your positive and intentional energy, make sure you take enough time to do it properly. You can check whether the pendulum is connected to your energy field before each session by spending 5-10 minutes sitting with it in your hands. Keep your eyes closed, breathe steadily, and just feel the energy going back and forth in your arm.

Some practitioners prefer to say a prayer or make an offering to their guides before beginning the divination. If you're working with a guide, this is also the best time to reach out to them. In case your preparation takes more than 15 minutes, you should consider taking out your pendulum only a minute or two before you're ready to use it. This will help you keep it safe and away from any source of negative energy so it remains a faithful extension of your intuition.

How to Get Started with Pendulum Dowsing

There are two fundamental principles in pendulum dowsing and divination itself. One is keeping an open mind, and the other is setting aside any judgment or preconceived notion you may have about the practice. As mentioned before, you won't get precise answers such as names, dates, or specific situations. So, to get the most accurate results possible, you'll need to keep an open mind about the messages you receive about the future. It's also possible to get several different answers for the same question or one answer that doesn't tell you anything about what you are interested in. This often happens to novices and only means you'll need to practice a bit more. However, the more open you are to the possibilities in the beginning, the easier you'll learn to interpret the messages. New practitioners often get stuck trying to decipher the information about the future simply because they focus on the answer already in their minds. You may assume you know the answer, but this isn't necessarily true. And the sooner you accept that the answer may differ from what you expect, the sooner you can get aligned with your future path.

Another mistake many novices make is expecting the pendulum to start swinging in clear directions right away. This rarely happens because your reflexes aren't yet in tune with the pendulum – even if your energy is. The pendulum must be under the influence of your reflexes for a while before it starts behaving as you would expect it. Maintain focus even if you don't feel you'll receive anything during the session. Keep your mind on your intention, but don't force it in the direction of any particular answer, as this could give you a false view of potential future outcomes.

Using your dominant hand to hold the pendulum when dowsing is a great way to get it aligned with your intuition. If you don't know which hand is your dominant hand, hold the pendulum in the one that feels more comfortable. You can try out both and see what your intuition tells you about which hand the pendulum feels closer to your higher being. The same goes for the length of the pendulum. To keep it close to you, use a shorter cord or chain, or simply wrap the excess around your forefinger. When you have prepared your mind, body, and space and brought your question into your focus, you can start dowsing using the following steps:

1. Sit in a comfortable position, and hold the pendulum between your index and thumb. Trace the length of the cord or chain with your other hand, stopping at the bottom of it with your palm facing upward.

2. Wait until the pendulum becomes still before moving your hand away from under it. If it starts moving again, don't worry, as this is entirely normal.

3. Relax your body by moving your shoulders back and straightening your spine. This also promotes energy flow through your body, making the messages more transparent.

4. Sit and watch the pendulum move until it stops again.

5. Now, you can start determining the proper responses you expect about what you're dowsing for.

6. Ask the pendulum a question you already know has a "yes" answer, and see how it moves. You can affirm this by repeatedly asking it to show you a "yes" message.

7. Repeat the same with a question that has a "no" for an answer. The question should be related to answers you can clearly see

without the need for dowsing. For example, if it's a Saturday, you can ask whether the next day will be Sunday.

8. If you still can't tell the difference between the responses, or if the pendulum changes the movement even with the same response, repeat the entire process as many times as necessary.

9. Once you've learned how to distinguish clearly between the "yes" and "no" answers, you'll be ready to ask more informative questions that can be answered with these. For example, you can ask the pendulum whether you'll find the item you want to buy on your next shopping trip.

It takes time to learn how to dowse confidently and find every bit of information you're looking for. As your confidence grows, you'll be able to ask more personal questions because you'll know that your intuition will always give you a reliable answer. You can also try specific exercises such as locating missing objects, pets, or places you've never been before. Just as the explorers dowse for water and precious metals in the future, so can you for exploring new areas near you. You'll need a simple map and hold the pendulum over it. After asking the questions, you observe the pendulum moving over specific parts of the map.

Practicing Divination with a Pendulum

This simple yet effective technique will help you understand your intuition and gain access to your subconscious thoughts. It will enable you to use your pendulum for divination. Here is how to do it:

1. Sit or stand in a comfortable position with your shoulders and body relaxed. There should be no tension in your arms or legs, either.

2. Place your hand palm up on a table, altar, or other sacred space in front of you, and take several deep breaths.

3. Take your time to relax, and perform breathing exercises, meditation, or other grounding techniques.

4. When you feel relaxed enough, ask the pendulum to show an affirmative answer in the same way as described in the dowsing section. Learning how to dowse is recommended first, as it helps you understand and calibrate the responses.

5. Wait until the pendulum starts moving, and you get a "yes" for an answer.

6. Repeat the process for the "no" answer by asking the pendulum for it.

7. You can now start asking simple yet specific questions. These may also serve you as a practice but can sometimes deliver a meaningful message.

8. You'll apply the same principle as you did with the dowsing techniques. The only exception is that all the questions (the practice and the main ones) should pertain to future outcomes and not something you want to find.

9. Finally, you should begin using the pendulum to gain insight into questions about the future. Again, start with a simple question. For example, you can ask whether it's a good idea to wear a particular outfit the next day. If the weather is expected to change, you'll probably get a negative answer.

10. As you practice this technique, you'll eventually learn to get answers to even more substantial questions – such as whether you should change jobs, relocate, continue your studies, and more.

Techniques and Tips for Developing Dowsing and Divination Skills

To get the best results and avoid misusing your pendulum, you should only use it when your mind frame is apt for dowsing or divination. Your emotions should be balanced and your thoughts controlled. It's a good idea to do a mental health check from time to time to ensure you remain motivated to keep honing your pendulum-wielding skills. If you aren't sure whether you're ready to use your pendulum, ask it. The tool will connect to your intuition and tell you right away if something is wrong.

While dowsing can be used to uncover potential health issues, including allergies, it should never replace a consultation with a medical professional. If you have a health concern, you should seek medical assistance as soon as possible. It's also a good idea to avoid dowsing for other people's health issues in the beginning. Once you can assert that you're skilled enough to perform this task, you may go ahead but only do it after gaining the other person's approval. You can use the pendulum to seek answers about someone else's future, but only if you have their permission. Be sure to explain to them the importance of keeping an open mind, as this will be necessary to align their energy with the pendulum and obtain an accurate reading.

Both pendulum dowsing and divination have limitations, which you and whomever your target should be aware of. Sometimes, it may be a good idea to consult other divination forms, especially if you're interested in learning how the past and present affect the future. However, pendulums will be the right way to go if you're only interested in clear affirmative or dissentient responses. That said, you shouldn't rely on pendulum dowsing to make decisions all the time. While you can use it to facilitate decision-making, it should never be your only driving force. Take responsibility for your actions, and start creating your own reality. Most importantly, if you change your behavior and the outcomes change, don't blame it on your tool if the newest development isn't to your liking.

What Can Affect Your Results?

Several factors may affect the results of pendulum dowsing and divination. Here are the most common ones:

The Force of Movement

The first and perhaps most decisive factor is the force your reflexes use to move the pendulum. This determines how forcefully the tool will move. For example, a strong swing in a predetermined direction (calibrated with the "yes" and "no" answers) signals a strong possibility of the message representing the truth. These types of responses are typically more reliable than the light swing in either direction. If the pendulum barely moves, this typically means the tool can't commit to giving you the answers. With dowsing, this can be caused by numerous factors. Meanwhile, a non-committal answer in divination usually means the outcome hasn't been determined yet.

Interpreting the Answers

Your ability to interpret the answers may also affect your capacity to find the answers you seek. Here is a great technique to practice if you want to see the answers more clearly:

1. Prepare your mind and focus it on the questions you need answers to.

2. Hold the pendulum in one hand and see how it swings while focusing on the questions even more intently.

3. Wait until the pendulum registers your energy. The time for this to happen varies. Sometimes, you'll get a quick response, while you need to wait a few minutes at other times. Be prepared for either possibility.

4. Think about how the pendulum signaled the response during the practice sessions or the previous time you used it for dowsing or divination.

5. Once you have your response, take your time to interpret it.

6. If you're uncertain whether you've got the correct response or seen it appropriately, ask another question from the pendulum. The more questions you ask, the better insight you'll gain into your topic of interest.

Relaxation

Your ability to relax is another essential aspect you may need to work on. While the steady rocking motion of the pendulum is designed to help you focus during the session, it doesn't always work perfectly. Sometimes, it excites the body so much that you simply lose focus on the task ahead. For maximum efficacy, you should be in a calm and neutral state of mind, which may require some work. Once that's achieved, the swaying or spinning motion of the pendulum will work wonders on seeping into your subconscious and accessing your intuitive wisdom.

Possible Issues with Pendulum Dowsing and Divination

There could be several reasons your pendulum may not offer accurate results when dowsing or looking into the future. Here are some of them:

- You haven't learned the proper language of your pendulum. Try practicing the "yes" and "no" responses again.

- You're too stressed to focus on your question or interpret the results correctly. Calm down before trying again.

- You have negative feelings or doubts about future outcomes even before seeing them. Make sure you dissipate these before interpreting the results.

- You may have electrical equipment disrupting the flow of energy around the pendulum. Use pendulums away from all gadgets and machines.

- Your pendulum hasn't been properly cleansed, charged, or programmed.

- Your questions aren't simple or specific enough, so you'll need to reformulate them.

- You haven't waited enough time. It may take more time for the question to reach its destination. Make sure you wait enough time for the answer to manifest itself.

- Your pendulum may not be aligned with your energy. Try finding a different one to see whether its energy is a better fit.

Chapter 7: Create a Pendulum Chart

When you hear the word pendulum, an image of a small sphere attached to a string, swaying left to right, landing on either "yes" or "no," comes to mind. Pendulum charts, however, extend the abilities of pendulums. They allow you to receive more complex answers than just "yes," "no," or "maybe." While using pendulum charts requires relatively more advanced skills, they can easily be learned with knowledge and practice.

Using a pendulum chart that suits your needs increases your likelihood of retrieving relevant information and guidance.

There are numerous types of pendulum charts, some more complex than others. While they may look different, they all operate in the same way. Yes or no pendulum charts use pre-programmed symbols. In other words, the chart has reference points that the pendulum uses to reveal the answers to your questions.

Using a pendulum chart that suits your needs increases your likelihood of retrieving relevant information and receiving guidance. Using the right pendulum chart allows you to ask more specific and detailed questions about several broader aspects of life. Suppose you use a pendulum chart that encompasses many possibilities. In that case, you can end up with information that you didn't even ask for in the first place. This is why people who have experience using pendulum charts are able to communicate more effectively with the divine.

Luckily, you can make pendulum charts at home easily. All you need is basic guidance and some common household materials. You need to follow very few rules when making a pendulum chart. Primarily, you'll have to rely on your intuition and imagination to come up with formats and keywords that will answer the questions that you have in mind.

This chapter covers everything you need to know about using and creating pendulum charts. You'll find out how to prepare yourself before working with a pendulum chart to ensure a fruitful experience. You'll also learn about the different types of pendulum charts and how to create and work with each one.

Before You Start

Before we can delve into making and using pendulum charts, you must find out how to prepare yourself for this process.

Center Yourself

Centering yourself before working with a pendulum chart is essential. Otherwise, you won't receive answers to the questions you direct at the pendulum. This is because you don't receive answers from the pendulum itself. It's an inanimate object, which is why your subconscious mind will not comprehend how or why you're trying to obtain answers from an object that lacks consciousness.

When working with a pendulum, you must instead direct your question to your higher self. Centering yourself allows you to shift your focus toward this intention. Start by finding a quiet place where you can work without any distractions. It's best to dedicate a space or corner of your home to divination practices, as we've explained in a previous chapter. This can be the spot that you always turn to whenever you need to center yourself. Make it as comfortable as you desire. You can use a mat, light up a few candles, or even place a comfortable chair and coffee table.

It also helps to burn incense or diffuse relaxing essential oils. That said, make sure that the decor and lighting aren't too stimulating for the senses. Tailoring the environment to your needs allows you to feel calm and at peace and encourages you to use it for other soothing purposes, such as meditating or reading.

Shift your focus to your breathing, keeping it as slow and steady as possible. Draw in deep breaths, releasing all the tension from your body as you exhale. Visualize the worry, stress, and anxiety exiting your body with each breath you take. Keep your focus there for a few minutes before moving on to meditation techniques.

Choose any meditation practice that you feel comfortable working with. Many people like to use the chakra harmonizing visualization technique, where you picture a white light engulfing you. You can also go for any simple breathing exercise that allows you to enter a relaxed state.

Come up with "Yes" or "No" Questions

Now that you feel appeased and grounded, think of the questions you wish to ask. Make sure they're focused, concise, simple, and clear. Start with questions that only require "yes" or "no" answers. Write down all the questions you want to ask on a piece of paper and test the pendulum before moving on to more complex charts. Make sure to include some questions to which you already know the answer, such as "Am I a woman?" "Is tomorrow Sunday?" and "Do I live with my parents?"

Reframe Your Thoughts

It's normal to feel confused when you're still learning to use the pendulum. You may experience difficulty getting your pendulum to move and give you an answer. Even if it does, you may doubt the response and wonder if it was a mere coincidence. Some people worry that their ego is what prompts the movement of the pendulum rather than their higher self. Others experience no difficulties getting the pendulum to swing right away. Ultimately, your ability to receive a response is directly associated with your headspace. This is why saying positive affirmations can help you get rid of any beliefs and preconceived notions that may be holding you back. Reframing your thoughts and maintaining a positive mindset are essential when practicing divination techniques.

Practicing the following steps will help you avoid any troubles throughout the process:

Step 1: Visualization

Start visualizing a large ball of light on top of your head. The bright, golden-white light is a symbol of your higher self and your superconscious mind. Imagine it growing larger, connecting your crown chakra and your third eye to your head.

Step 2: Recite Releasing Statements

This isn't just about repeating them loudly. You have to believe in what you're saying. To do that, stand in a private space, speak slowly and articulately, and take the time to savor and feel your words as if they were really happening. Maintain a positive mindset throughout the process.

Releasing statements can help you get rid of any limiting beliefs. They allow you to let go of those fears that you hold deep within your subconscious mind. These convictions and worries block you from moving forward and prevent you from learning the truth from your spirit guides and higher self.

The following are some releasing statements that you can recite:

- I allow myself to let go of all judgment, perception, and conviction that I am fearful of working with my higher self and superconscious mind to unlock the truth.

- I choose to get rid of the need to believe that I am afraid to work with my higher self and superconscious mind.

- I release all judgment, perception, and conviction that learning the truth will harm me and others.

- I release all judgment, perception, and conviction that I am anxious about learning the truth.

- I let go of all judgment, perception, and conviction that dowsing with a pendulum to know the truth is challenging.

- I choose to let go of the need to believe that dowsing with a pendulum to know the truth is challenging.

- I release all judgment, perception, and conviction that I will receive wrong answers if I work with my higher self using a pendulum.

Any thoughts and beliefs that are actively released from your subconscious mind should always be replaced with a positive statement. This is why you should always recite replacing statements as well.

Step 3: Recite Replacing Statements

Reciting and replacing statements loudly with conviction, clear intention, and focus is vital in rewiring your brain. This makes working with a pendulum chart and your higher self significantly easier.

The following are some replacement statements that you can recite:

- I now command my subconscious mind to wholly believe and accept that I can receive accurate answers and helpful guidance from my superconscious mind and higher self by using a pendulum chart.

- I believe I am always optimistic when working with my superconscious mind and higher self when performing pendulum dowsing.

- I know exactly what it feels like to be working with my superconscious mind and higher self with conviction, belief, positivity, and trust.

- I fully comprehend how it feels to use pendulum charts and pendulum dowsing as an effective means of communication with my spirit guides and higher self. I do it with trust, conviction, and positivity.

- I find it effortless to use pendulums and pendulum charts to communicate with my superconscious mind and higher self to obtain beneficial answers to my questions.

Types of Pendulum Charts

Pendulum charts come in numerous shapes and forms. You can find printable templates online for diverse purposes. However, learning how to make your own charts allows you to personalize them and tailor them to your needs. Creating your own pendulum charts enables you to ask more specific questions and yield accurate answers.

In this section, you'll find step-by-step instructions on creating each type of pendulum chart, from the simple "Yes" or "No" charts to more complex ones. You'll come to understand when and how to use each of these charts.

"Yes" or "No" Pendulum Chart

You can use this chart to ask simple and direct questions that require yes/no answers. As mentioned previously, you should start your pendulum dowsing or divination session with these types of questions to ensure that you're actively communicating with your higher self.

How to Make the Pendulum Chart

Grab a standard-sized paper and a pen or pencil. Keep the paper in a portrait perspective (not landscape). In the middle of the paper, draw a small circle on the left side and another on the right using a protractor. Draw an oblong box at the bottom center and another at the top. Write the word "yes" in the circle on the left and the word "no" in the other circle. Write the word "maybe" in the oblong box at the bottom and the words "not at this time" in the other oblong.

How to Use the Pendulum Chart

Remind yourself of the intention of the ball of white golden light on top of you being connected to your higher self. With this intention in mind, follow these steps:

1. Use your consciousness to swing the pendulum from front to back. Say, "This means a "yes" answer."
2. Use your consciousness to swing the pendulum from left to right. Say, "This means a "no" answer."

3. Repeat both steps until you're confident that these answers have been established.

4. Ask the following questions:

- "Higher self, am I a woman?"
- "Higher self, am I a man?"

The pendulum should move towards either the "yes" or "no," depending on the correct answer. The pendulum should still give you a satisfactory answer if you identify as neither a man nor a woman.

Don't fret if it doesn't move in the right direction right away. Keep practicing several times until you get the correct answer. Always direct the question to your higher self and not to the pendulum or your ego self.

Half Shape Pendulum Chart

Half shape pendulum charts are typically used to ask relationship-related questions. However, you can use them to ask about a broad range of subjects.

How to Make the Pendulum Chart

Grab a standard-size sheet of paper and use it from a landscape perspective. Draw an upwards half-circle across the entire width and length of the paper. Draw a smaller half-circle within it, leaving enough space to write between both boundaries.

- ### Relationship Pendulum Chart

Divide the space between both half-circles into four equal sections. Write each of these words in an individual section: "physical," "spiritual," "mental," and "emotional."

Divide the area inside the small half-circle into three equal sections. Write each of these words in an individual section: "short," "medium," and "long."

- ### Numbered Pendulum Chart

Divide the half-circles into ten equal sections. Use the space between them to number each section from 10 to 100 percent in increments of ten (10%, 20%, 30%, 40%, etc.).

- ### Multiple Choice Pendulum Chart

Use this pendulum chart if you're stuck between several choices. You can divide it into as many sections as you like. Say you picked out five restaurant options, but you're struggling to choose one for your upcoming date. In that case, you'll split the chart into five sections, writing the name of one restaurant in each of the sections.

How to Use the Pendulum Chart

• Relationship Pendulum Chart

Ask the following questions:

1. What type of relationship is this?

The pendulum should swing along the four sections between both half-circles before it lands on an answer.

2. How long will we be together?

The pendulum should swing along the three sections in the smaller half-circle before it lands on an answer.

• Numbered Pendulum Chart

Ask questions that require numerical or percent-based answers. Start by asking: How accurate is this pendulum?

You may want to balance the pendulum depending on the answer you receive.

• Multiple Choice Pendulum Chart

Ask your questions and wait for the pendulum to land on the answers.

For example, if you're trying to decide on a restaurant, you can ask the following questions:

1. Which of these restaurants serves the best food?
2. Which of these restaurants has the best ambiance?
3. Which of these restaurants offers the best value for money?
4. Which of these restaurants has the highest hygienic standards?

Full Shape Pendulum Chart

Last but not least, this type of chart can be used to answer very specific questions in a wide range of subjects.

How to Make the Pendulum Chart

Use a protractor to draw a circle on a standard-size sheet of paper. Keeping the paper in a portrait perspective, make the circle as large as possible. Draw a smaller circle inside. Draw a line down the center of the circles, splitting them in half. Divide each of the circles into as many sections as you like. The sections on the upper left side of the circle are called "inside chart left," and the others are called "outside chart left." The sections in the upper right side of the circle are called "inside chart right," and the others are called "outside chart right."

How to Use the Pendulum Chart

When using this chart, begin by asking for general answers before moving on to more specific ones. Let's say you're still choosing between restaurants, only this time, you're choosing between four cuisines and 16 different restaurants (four restaurants for each cuisine).

In that case, you'll split the area between the boundaries of both circles into 4 equal sections. You can write the words "Italian," "Japanese," "Mediterranean," and "Chinese" (one in each section). You'll split the smaller circle into 16 equal sections and write the names of four Italian restaurants in the sections below the word "Italian," four Japanese restaurants in the sections below the word "Japanese," and so on.

Then, you'll ask the pendulum questions like:

1. Which of these cuisines has the healthiest food?

2. Which of these cuisines uses most of my favorite ingredients?

Once you settle on a cuisine, you can ask questions that will allow you to choose between the corresponding restaurants.

Congratulations! You now know everything you need to do to prepare yourself for this divination technique. You also know how to create and use various types of pendulum charts. This knowledge is bound to serve you as you keep developing your pendulum-wielding skills. Now, you're ready to move on to using the pendulum for spiritual healing.

Chapter 8: Pendulums for Spiritual Healing

This chapter explores the practice of spiritual energy healing using a pendulum in more depth. You'll understand how to use a pendulum as a diagnostic, cleansing, and healing tool. Upon reading this chapter, you'll learn how to scan the body and check the status of your chakras using the pendulum. You'll also find out how to incorporate this tool into Reiki practices and how to use it to balance your chakras.

The energy flow generated by the chakras is amplified by the pendulum.
https://pixabay.com/es/photos/p%c3%a9ndulo-p%c3%a9ndulo-de-oro-reflexi%c3%b3n-686680/

Scanning the Body with a Pendulum

Pendulums are among the best tools to scan the body and determine the state of the chakras. This is because the pendulum amplifies the energy flow generated by the chakras. You can get a sense of the state of your chakras by observing the way that the pendulum swings – its movement is a manifestation of the energy produced by each chakra.

What Is the Chakra System?

The chakra system holds the "prana," or energy, in the body. The word "chakra" is Sanskrit for disk or wheel, which makes sense because, according to Ayurvedic medicine, the chakras are wheels of energy that can be found at several points along the body. While we have 114 chakras in total, the seven main chakras are located along the spine. They start at its base, extending all the way to the crown of the head.

Our behaviors, feelings, thoughts, experiences, and memories affect the chakras' energy. They directly impact our current and future physical, mental, social, and emotional health. We are at our healthiest when all our chakras are unblocked. This is because open chakras enable the free flow of energy throughout the body. When this occurs, our mind, body, and spirit exist in harmony.

Our chakras are constantly opening and closing, depending on our feelings, thoughts, and dynamics of life. These energy centers are constantly trying to align with the changing energy flows.

How to Check the Status of Your Chakras with a Pendulum

You can do several things to check on the state of your chakras using a pendulum. Here are some of the methods you can use:

Ask for Help

To use this method, you'll need a pendulum and the help of another person. The pendulum doesn't have to be programmed, but before you start, you must be clear about who will direct your questions. Both of you should start by meditating or practicing mindfulness techniques. You must have a clear mind and no expectations whatsoever.

To start off, you need to lie down on your back. Ask your helper to hold the pendulum just a few inches over your body. Have them hold it above each chakra for as long as they need to observe the pendulum's motion. They should write down the direction of the swinging of the chakra. When they've finished, turn over on your stomach and ask them to repeat the process.

Compare the first and second readings and watch out for any differences. Notice the force of the swing and its direction for each of the chakras. The greater the swing, the more energy is in that chakra. Ideally, you want all your chakras to be open and generate equally comparable swings. That said, chances are you'll find discrepancies between each chakra from both sets of readings.

Taking the time to determine these differences can help you identify the imbalances in your body and the problems you need to address. Here is a guide you can use to determine what each pendulum swing means:

- **Clockwise:** Open chakra, balanced, and free-flowing energy
- **Counterclockwise:** Closed chakra, out of balance, and restricted or blocked energy flow
- **A Straight Line in Either Direction:** Partially closed or open chakra, imbalance, and partial blockage of energy flow
- **Elliptical:** An imbalance in the right or left side of the chakra, which can be out of balance on either side while energy is still flowing
- **No Movement:** Blocked chakra, no flow of energy, or full blockage.

Use the Chakra Symbols as a Proxy

Suppose you don't wish to ask for someone's help. In that case, you can check your chakra's status using any pendulum and a colored printout that includes the symbol of each of the seven chakras. Declare who you're asking your questions to, whether they're your spirit guides, superconscious mind, or higher self. Clear your mind by performing breathing exercises or any mindfulness technique of your choice.

The colored printout will represent your own chakras. Rest the paper on a table and start only when you're in the right headspace. Hold the pendulum a few inches over each symbol. Visualize each area of your body during the whole process. For example, visualize your lower back or spine as you hold the pendulum over the root chakra symbol.

Many people accidentally visualize the answer to the pendulum – you should be careful not to do this. Write down your observations regarding the size and direction of the pendulum swing, and use the guide above to interpret your readings.

Use a Pendulum Chart

You can also print out a chakra pendulum chart to scan your body. The pendulum you use doesn't need to be programmed. If you don't have a printer, use the previous chapter as a guide on creating your own pendulum chart.

Create a half shape chart and divide it into seven equal half-circle sections. In the space between the boundaries of each half-circle, write the names of the chakras (each in a different section). You can color each section with the color of its corresponding chakra. If you can, draw each symbol or cut and paste tiny printouts of the symbols. In the smaller half-circle, you may write the name of each chakra in Sanskrit and the areas they affect. For example, in the root chakra section, you may write Muladhara and grounding, balance, stability, nourishment, strength, physical health, family, security, etc.

Clear your mind using a mindfulness technique (you may use the golden white light visualization technique from the previous chapter), and be clear about who you're directing your questions to. Place the chart on a desk and hold the pendulum over the center of the chart.

Ask your higher self or superconscious mind specific questions like:

1. Which of the chakras is open?
2. Which of the chakras holds the highest energy today?
3. Which of the chakras do I need to pay attention to the most?
4. Which of the chakras is contributing to my anxiety today?
5. Which of the chakras has a restricted flow of energy?

Your questions should be concise and straightforward enough to elicit a helpful answer from the pendulum. For example, you cannot ask vague questions like "What is the state of my chakras?"

Observe the swinging of the pendulum. If you ask it about your closed chakras, it will swing through the chakras that need the most attention, then stop or return to the root chakra it moved toward. If you ask which of your chakras are open and it swings clockwise, then all your chakras are open. By contrast, a counterclockwise movement indicates that all your chakras are closed.

Using a Pendulum in Reiki

If you wish to do reiki, relying on the pendulum is not advised throughout the entire healing session. Reiki healing is all about maintaining a connection with the person you're practicing with. Using a pendulum and paying attention to its movement throughout the entire session can prevent you from doing so.

Using a pendulum at the beginning of a reiki healing session allows you to identify the person's needs. It also helps you to determine if all the issues are addressed during the session. Pendulums are mainly used in reiki for two purposes: to determine each chakra's status and identify the crystals that should be used in the session.

What Is Reiki?

Reiki is a form of energy healing that can help induce tranquility and relaxation. This traditional Japanese technique aims to reduce anxiety and stress. Reiki practitioners rely on their hands and gentle touch to transmit energy to your body. This enhances the flow of energy and promotes balance, which encourages healing.

Reiki is a complementary, holistic healing technique focusing on emotional, mental, physical, and spiritual aspects. It can help bring the body to a meditative state and stimulate self-healing. This healing technique supports one's general well-being by strengthening the immune system, alleviating physical and emotional pain, relieving tension, and even promoting the healing of bones and tissues after serious injuries or surgery.

Individuals who undergo rigorous treatments like dialysis, surgery, radiation, and chemotherapy often turn to reiki for support. This medical and therapeutic treatment instills feelings of peace, security, wellness, and relaxation. That said, it's not considered an alternative medicine technique because it can't be a substitute for traditional treatments. It mainly accelerates the healing process and makes medical treatments more efficient.

Regular reiki sessions can keep you healthy if you don't struggle with particular ailments. They serve as good preventative medical techniques to help you deal with stress more efficiently.

Reiki practitioners act as a middleman between you and the main source of the prana, the ultimate universal life force. They use their hands to deliver this energy to your body. Your body is smart enough to accept only the amount of energy needed to thrive – it doesn't matter what the reiki master believes you need.

How to Use a Pendulum in a Reiki Healing Session

Even if you aren't a reiki master or practitioner, you can still practice this technique with a friend. Try to take it lightly, and don't forget to enjoy it, especially if you're new to this healing method. None of us maintain perfectly balanced chakras at all times, which is entirely normal.

Don't panic if the pendulum swings counterclockwise, indicating a blocked chakra. Freaking out will only cause your friend to worry even though they're fine. A blocked chakra indicates that your friend is experiencing a rough patch in life or is lacking some guidance and a sense of purpose. Fortunately, using a pendulum in reiki can help you determine the type of healing crystal your friend needs to promote a better flow of energy and restore balance to their chakra system.

Follow these practical steps if you wish to use a pendulum in a reiki session:

Step 1: Ask your friend to lie down on their back with their eyes closed. Tell them to draw in a couple of deep breaths and encourage them to clear their minds. If needed, you can walk them through guided meditation or breathing exercises. Have them call in their higher self. As a practitioner, you should also do the same – call in your healing or spirit guides and your higher self.

Step 2: Hold the pendulum a few inches over each of the seven chakras. Pause at each one for a moment to ask if this chakra is open. For example, you can ask, "Is (your friend's name) root chakra open?"

Step 3: As you ask each question, lightly swing the pendulum clockwise. Allow it to settle freely in any direction that it wants after you rotate it. In addition to the guide provided earlier in this chapter, you can use the direction of the swing to determine the degree of openness or closedness. For instance, if you get a 45-degree swing, this would indicate that the chakra is half open. An 80-degree swing, on the other hand, suggests that the chakra is mostly open. Use 90 degrees as your ceiling.

Follow these instructions to draw a chart that you can use for guidance:

1. Draw a vertical line down the center of the paper.
2. Draw a horizontal line halfway through the first line.
3. You should be left with what looks like the coordinate plane you used to draw in math class.
4. Draw a diagonal line that cuts through the middle of the first and third quadrants (upper right side to lower left side of the plane).
5. Draw another diagonal line that cuts through the middle of the second and fourth quadrants (upper left side to lower right side of the plane).
6. You should now have 8 equal sections.

   - The pendulum moving along the vertical line indicates a healthy or open chakra.
   - If the pendulum moves along the horizontal line, this indicates a closed or unhealthy chakra.
   - If the pendulum moves along the first diagonal line (upper right to lower left), this indicates a 50% open, overactive chakra.
   - If the pendulum moves along the second diagonal line (upper left to lower right), this indicates a 50% open, underactive chakra.

Now that you have a visual of the chart, memorize the directions and hold the pendulum directly over your friend's chakra. Only use the chart as a reference if you need it.

If you're a reiki practitioner, you should always ask your client if there's something they'd like to address during the healing session. Also, ask them if there's something you need to know about their current mental, emotional, spiritual, and physical state of health. Make sure to do that only after you use your intuition to determine the status of the chakras, as any upfront knowledge can lead to biased results. The energies in certain aspects of our lives manifest as imbalances in the chakras. For example, if a person struggles with relationships, they must work on their sacral and heart chakras.

After you've determined the status of the chakras, use the pendulum to determine which healing crystal to use.

What Are Healing Crystals?

When used correctly, healing crystals can deliver the powerful healing energy of the Earth. They generate positive and energizing vibrations that promote peace of mind and allow you to feel more energetic.

You can use numerous healing crystals, each of which uniquely affects the mind, body, and spirit. The vibrations emitted by each crystal are determined by how its molecules and atoms are arranged and how they interact and move.

Since our bodies are dynamic, complex, and electromagnetic, we always have spiritual, physical, mental, and emotional energy fields flowing through and around us. This means that crystals' energies and vibrations can affect us when they interact with our energy fields.

How to Use a Pendulum to Choose a Crystal to Work With

Using a pendulum to determine which healing crystal to work with is a very easy feat. Here is how you can do it:

Step 1: Arrange your healing crystals on a flat surface.

Step 2: Ask your higher self to guide you toward those it believes will benefit your friend (or client) the most.

Step 3: Gently hold the pendulum over your crystal collection and search for and observe its movement. Your intuition and indicators from the pendulum will help you to choose the right crystal.

Step 4: You must trust that your higher self and spirit guide will guide you toward the right crystal for this to work.

Balancing the Chakras with a Pendulum

Besides determining the status of your chakras, you can also use a pendulum to balance your chakra system. Here's how you can do it:

Cleansing Your Pendulum

You must cleanse your pendulum before you use it in any healing or balancing work. You also need to do this if you decide to work with crystals. This can help you get rid of any blockages and negative vibrations. It allows you to deliver the right message to your body effectively.

As you've seen, you can cleanse your pendulum or crystal via smudging. You can also run it underwater, allow it to recharge under the full moon or sunlight, or bury it in soil. If you plan to use sunlight to recharge your pendulum or crystal, make sure not to leave it there too long, as it may hinder its function.

In parallel, ensure you're ready before working with a pendulum. Take a couple of deep breaths and practice some visualization or grounding techniques. You can meditate for a while or retreat to a quiet spot. Do whatever it takes to put your thoughts on mute, disconnect from the external world, and get in touch with your deeper self. When you're ready, you can start balancing your chakras.

How to Balance the Chakras with a Pendulum

Hold the pendulum over each of your chakras in order. The pendulum will begin to show you the state of each of your chakras. Once that's done, go back to your root chakra and start moving along each of your chakras again. Use your intuition and the pendulum's swinging to determine how long you should stay above each energy center.

Make sure that your intention is clear – inviting all your chakras to fall into balance and harmony. Harmony, in essence, is the universe's natural frequency. You don't need to do anything except ask and allow your body to heal itself. Trust in its wisdom to do so.

If you're practicing on someone else, you must get them to trust in their body's ability to heal itself. You can do that by talking to them about what each chakra represents as you hold the pendulum over them. Explain their functions and how they work. That way, your friend or client will eventually let go of any mental blockages and believe in their self-healing powers.

Even though the pendulum is widely known as a diagnostic tool, you can simply use it to balance your chakras by asking your body to balance itself. Acknowledging your body's wisdom and power is enough to stimulate realignment. Once you believe you've addressed all these issues, return to the root chakra and start moving along the energy centers one last time. Make sure they're all open and that the pendulum is swinging in the same direction and with the same level of force for each of them. Don't worry if you don't receive the desired results right away. The more you practice working with pendulums and trusting your intuition, the easier and more enjoyable it will get.

Our bodies are more powerful than we could ever realize. We don't need to rely on other people and tools to feel balanced and at peace. Practicing reiki and working with pendulums stimulates and supports the natural self-healing abilities of the human body.

Chapter 9: Enhancing Your Pendulum Intuition

The world of divination is vast and versatile, involving various practices, including pendulum reading. While these practices may differ from one another, they share the same foundation. To truly practice the art of divination, you need to be in touch with your intuition. You must be aware of the energies surrounding you and how they affect everything around you. Being in touch with your intuition means listening to it and trusting it.

To truly practice the art of divination, you need to be in touch with your intuition.
https://pixabay.com/es/photos/p%c3%a9ndulo-mapa-navegaci%c3%b3n-br%c3%bajula-1934311/

Intuition is key when practicing divination. You can theoretically learn how to read and use the pendulum, but your readings will lack accuracy and flavor if you're not using your intuition. Intuition is what separates practitioners from each other – everyone is different, and so is their intuition. One practitioner's intuition may highlight certain elements in your readings, while others might pick on different aspects. You may also receive the same reading from different interpreters, but each of them will explain it in their own way. In other words, everyone's intuition is unique. This is why every reading has its own flavor and style.

By the end of this chapter, you'll have garnered plenty of useful insights to develop your intuition and enhance your magical or spiritual practice using the pendulum.

What Is Intuition?

Intuition is a widely known and accepted term. You must have heard about intuition if you're familiar with any spiritual practice. Many people know about intuition or are familiar with the general meaning, but not everyone knows exactly what intuition entails.

Simply put, intuition is the voice that emanates from your higher self. Your higher self is connected to your soul, which is in tune with the universe. This means that once you unlock your intuition, you'll learn how to pick up on the universe's waves and messages. You'll learn how to be in harmony with the universe and achieve your soul's purpose.

Listening to your intuition is a sacred and divine practice. Acting according to your intuition harmonizes you with the energy of the universe. Being in harmony with the universe will make you feel at home, which is one of the main reasons you should practice listening to your higher self's voice. Besides, unlocking your intuition should be a priority if you want to become a pendulum interpreter.

Intuition is like a muscle. The more you use and maintain it, the stronger it gets. Strong intuition allows for accurate readings and sharp gut instincts. This muscle is located in your third eye chakra, also known as the Anja.

The Anja is the center of your intuition. It is the sixth chakra and is located in the center of your forehead. Anja is known as the pineal gland. Scientifically, the pineal gland is a small part of your brain responsible for the intuitive messages you receive. Knowing where the center is, is important because once you do, it becomes easier to activate your intuition and tap into it.

Listening to Your Intuition

Now that you know what intuition is, it's time to know what it feels and sounds like. Your intuition is a voice that comes from within you. It feels calm, serene, and certain. It is common to confuse intuition with the sound of reason or the nagging voice of anxiety, but it is neither one of those things. When your intuition speaks to you, you'll feel like it has a sense of knowing. This voice will not nag you or make you feel like you should do something the way anxiety does. The more you trust and develop it, the better you'll become at differentiating it from other voices.

Now, you may wonder how to listen to it, especially if you haven't mindfully chosen to listen to your intuition before. It is normal not to be sure at first. Hopefully, this chapter will guide and introduce you to various methods to help you listen to your higher self's voice.

In the meantime, one of the simplest ways to receive guidance with intuition is to ask the universe. Set your intention on unlocking your intuition, which will enable you to put out energy into the universe. The universe will respond by giving you guidance. This guidance may take many forms, but you'll know it when you see it. It is also vital to know that acting on your intentions is another way of putting energy into the universe. Remember that whatever you put into the universe will come back to you. Setting your intentions is not enough – your actions need to mirror them, too.

Intuition and Pendulum Reading

By now, you know how to use the pendulum and are aware of different methods you can use to practice interpreting the pendulum. You know how the pendulum gives you an answer and how it swings.

You may ask yourself why you need to be in tune with your intuition if the pendulum is there to give you the necessary answers. That is a fair question. In reality, interpreting the pendulum without listening to your intuition may not always result in accurate readings or in readings that make sense.

Sometimes, the universe, energies, and the supernatural realm speak to us in a language we may not understand. Your intuition is your translator, guiding you in deciphering the message that you receive from a pendulum reading. You may receive a visual message or experience a certain feeling when interpreting your pendulum. These messages your intuition picks up on may not appear as clearly through your pendulum.

The more you use your pendulum, the more you'll become familiar with it. You will notice that your pendulum moves differently every time you use it. You may not understand the pendulum's movement if you're not in tune with your intuition. This means you won't be able to decipher its response. So, your intuition is the main tool that will help you retrieve and correctly interpret your pendulum's answers. You'll be able to distinguish weak pendulum motions from stronger ones. You'll be able to understand your pendulum's "yes," "no," and "maybe" without using a chart.

Remember that your intuition will set you apart from other pendulum users. This isn't to say that certain users are better than others. However, every practitioner has their own unique style. Pendulum interpreters add their own flavor to their readings when they allow their intuition to guide them. This is why reading with intuition is essential and does not solely depend on the pendulum's movements. Ultimately, the input that your intuition offers is valuable and essential.

Scientific Studies on Intuition

The world abounds with skeptics who believe intuition is just another new-age spiritual nonsense. That is fair because, at the end of the day, many people find it difficult to believe in the unseen. Fortunately, numerous studies have targeted intuition to determine whether it exists and to understand it scientifically.

According to Dr. Lou Cozolino, science gives a clear explanation of intuition and gut instincts. Cozolino explains that these intuitive messages are a product of channels and neurons that process information in the brain.

As neuroscientist Antonio Damasio explains, intuition is a product of evolution. He refers to intuition as "somatic markers," arguing that the more humans evolve, the more their brains grow somatic markers that help them understand subconscious emotions, read the environment around them, and make quick decisions. Damasio explains that intuition has helped humans survive, increased their chances of survival, and avoided perilous outcomes.

Dr. Daryl Bem, an American psychologist, conducted a study with 1000 participants. Bem designed different experiments to understand intuition and study its functions. He found that human beings can sense something before it occurs. He also stated that, although humans do not have the ability to predict the future, they can feel it before it manifests in the physical world.

Dr. Bem told Cornell News that he doesn't know how humans have developed these sensitive antennas capable of feeling events before they occur. He further explained that intuition helps humans make faster decisions and boosts their chances of making better choices that are in tune with what is best for them.

The assistant clinical professor of psychiatry at UCLA, Dr. Judith Orloff, theorized that intuition is part of the brain's hippocampus and is connected to the gut. She states that maintaining a healthy gut is essential for clearer, intuitive messages.

Dr. Orloff states that paying attention to literal gut feelings is vital. For example, if you feel off around a certain person, then you should take it as a warning sign. This sign is your intuition telling you that it may be best not to interact with that person or trust them. Orloff claims that trusting these feelings can help you avoid many problems and negative outcomes. Additionally, she works with women who wish to develop their intuition. These women view their intuition as their supernatural power that aids them in becoming better leaders and making better decisions.

How to Unlock and Maintain Your Intuition

There are numerous methods you can use to access and develop your intuition. Of course, these methods are spiritual and will significantly add to your life. Not only will they help you with your intuition, but they'll also support your spiritual awakening journey. Generally speaking, there is no specific method you should stick to. What matters is to feel comfortable with whichever method or methods you choose.

Meditation

Silencing the mind is essential when it comes to listening to your intuition. This will help you discern your higher self's voice from others. In that regard, meditation will sharpen your focus and help clear your mental environment. The clearer your mind is, the easier it will be to feel centered and listen to your intuition clearly.

Multiple meditation techniques are designed to help you connect with your third eye. That said, checking in with yourself before you pick a meditation practice is important. Read about each of them to determine which one you would like to try first. If you're unsure which one to start with, try all of them. Once you do, you'll be able to decide which ones you want to use.

Remember that when it comes to spiritual practices, you must practice the methods you are most comfortable with. Meditation shouldn't make you feel anxious or pressured in any way. That said, you need to be emotionally aware enough when you are meditating. Practice what serves you, and simply discard the rest.

Mantra Meditation

Mantra meditation revolves around repeating the same word or sentence. Your intention is essential with this type of meditation. You'll be setting all your focus and energy on this one mantra which will act according to your intention. So, before you meditate, be sure to set your intention clearly.

Think of what you'll learn from this type of meditation. The outcome should be related to enhancing your intuition, so set your intentions and meditate. Pick a mantra and stick to it – you can pick any one. Here are some mantras you can use or draw inspiration from you to create your own:

- I clearly hear my intuition
- My intuition speaks to me
- I am in tune with my intuition
- I believe in my ability to develop my intuition
- My intuition will guide me toward greater spiritual horizons

There are no strict rules regarding how long you should meditate. The important thing is to take deep breaths as you meditate and refocus when you experience brain chatter, also known as the "monkey brain." If this happens to you, gently guide your focus onto your mantra. Be kind to yourself when you do this. Frustration may inevitably interrupt your flow, so do your best to maintain your balance and stay grounded.

Visualization Meditation

This type of meditation relies on the power of visualization. To visualize an image in your brain is to clearly paint a picture of your goal. Try to live the image you are seeing in your head. Feel what it would be like to live according to your image. For instance, as you try to unlock your intuition, picture yourself acting according to your intuition. Feel the peace and calmness that come with listening to this voice. Picture yourself living in harmony with yourself and the universe. Envision yourself interpreting accurate readings thanks to your intuition.

Focus on this imagery as you meditate. Again, you can meditate as long as you see fit. However, you should know that as a beginner, or if you haven't meditated in a while, it's best to meditate for short periods at a time. Begin with five minutes, then ten minutes, until you find a duration that effectively brings you closer to your deeper self and connects you with your intuition.

Crystals

Crystals are formed by Mother Nature. While they may have different energies, they're all pure and positive in nature. Each crystal boasts various properties and radiates different energies. This is why specific crystals react with certain wavelengths, making them suitable for a wide range of magical or spiritual practices.

This means that certain crystals vibrate and resonate with your own intuition. In other words, certain kinds of crystals can help you unlock your intuition and be in tune with it. Since Mother Nature is so gracious, you can choose from plenty of crystals to enhance your intuitive powers. For a refresher, these include:

- Labradorite
- Amethyst
- Lapis lazuli

- Purple fluorite
- Azurite
- Kyanite
- Sodalite
- Lepidolite
- Lolite
- Citrine
- Turquoise
- Black Obsidian
- Black Tourmaline
- Clear Quartz

Crystals work through connection and reciprocated energy. When choosing a crystal to develop your intuition, make sure that you feel connected to it first before using it. This connection might manifest as an attraction to a certain type, or one or several crystals may stand out to you. Experiment with these and check in with your feelings and intuition. Ask the universe for guidance and observe yourself to see which crystal sparks a feeling within you.

Once you've picked a crystal, as we've mentioned before, you'll need to cleanse it. You can do so with sound, incense, or water. You know that certain crystals can be prone to degradation if exposed to water or moisture, so make sure you select an appropriate type. Next comes the charging phase, which you can do through sunlight or moonlight or by burying it in soil.

Now that your crystal is charged, you may use it. Hold your crystal between your palms and speak your intention into it. Tell the crystal what you wish to have. For instance, tell it that you want to hear your intuition clearly or need help unlocking your third eye. Thank your crystal for its gifts, and keep it around you. You can wear it as jewelry or keep it next to you when you're meditating.

Ultimately, your intuition plays a major role when interpreting the pendulum or practicing divination. If you want to become a pendulum interpreter, then you must work on your intuition. Accessing your intuition is neither difficult nor impossible. You have everything it takes to unlock this voice within you. Understand that this voice has always been a part of you. Every method or activity you'll perform will help you find this voice. These methods will help you learn how to listen to your intuition and how to differentiate it from other voices. They will sharpen your higher self's voice, providing you with clarity and confidence for your magical or spiritual practice.

Give yourself the grace and kindness you deserve as you learn about and develop your intuition. Do not succumb to feelings of frustration or demotivation when you don't achieve the desired results right away. Keep in mind that enhancing your intuition is an ongoing journey, so it's important to practice, be consistent, and allow yourself enough time until you reach your spiritual destination. Hopefully, the knowledge and tips included in this chapter will enable you to tap into your full intuitive potential, which you'll employ to strengthen your pendulum practice.

Chapter 10: Pendulum Magic

The pendulum is one of the easiest divination tools you can use. Once you have learned its language and how to use it, everything becomes much easier in your journey. What's great is that there are no limits to what you can do with your pendulum – you can inquire about virtually anything you wish to know about.

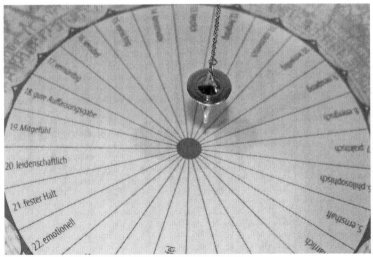

The pendulum is one of the easiest divination tools you can use.
https://pixabay.com/es/photos/p%c3%a9ndulo-paneles-de-p%c3%a9ndulo-tablero-242746/

As you know by now, there is magic in everything and everywhere around us. Pendulum magic is no different. You can use it with different divination tools and seek answers that you'll only find through the pendulum. This final chapter explores various methods and exercises you can engage in using the power of your pendulum.

Psychic Protection

It's always wise to protect yourself spiritually, regardless of whether or not you are a practitioner of the mystical. Think about it – you are mind, body, and soul. People spend time protecting their bodies from harm and do the same with their mental health, so why should it be any different for the soul?

Protecting yourself from psychic attacks is essential. If you're left unprotected, people can knowingly or unknowingly hurt you. If you believe in energies and how they work, you know that everyone is affected by the energies surrounding them. This means that a person can subconsciously send negative vibrations your way. Someone else may know exactly what they are doing and harm your energy on purpose.

Spiritualists always warn people about "psychic vampires." This term applies to those who feel rejuvenated after sucking the energy out of another person. Hopefully, you've never encountered a psychic vampire. Still, if you ever do, you must be prepared to ward off their negativity.

The Symptoms

To know whether you are being psychically attacked, you need to recognize what to look for. There are various ways in which an attack can show up, depending on who or what is attacking you. For instance, people who spend time around energy vampires usually feel significantly drained afterward. This pattern repeats itself until the person can connect the dots and understand what is happening to them. Other symptoms include low self-esteem and feeling unseen, unheard, and unworthy. While you may not feel all these symptoms at once, you'll feel like you have been energetically drained.

Other attacks may make you feel like you're always tired, constantly demotivated, and feeling low in general. These feelings will also be accompanied by daily nightmares, odd dreams, and experiencing bizarre circumstances. For example, you may suddenly feel the negative energy in the air or frequently find yourself in inextricable situations.

Protection

The Pendulum

Luckily, there are multiple ways to shield yourself from low-frequency energies. You can use the pendulum to identify the source of the attack. If there are people you are suspicious of, then write their names down on a dedicated chart and ask the pendulum to show you who is wishing harm upon you. You can also ask if this person is jealous of you, resents you, etc. After this part, you can proceed by asking the pendulum whether you should steer clear of certain people in your life.

Guard Your Aura

Shielding your aura is one of the best ways to protect your energy. Start by taking deep breaths, pausing, and then slowly exhaling. As you breathe in and out, imagine your aura growing in size. After that, take yourself out on a walk, or engage in an activity that benefits your aura. These can include laughing exercises, reading, working out, or getting a massage. Do whatever you feel the day calls for, as long as it strengthens your aura.

Crystals and Light Circles

According to psychics and energy healers, the bottom four chakras are most affected when people are energetically attacked. You can protect these areas by wearing crystals. Now, before you do, make sure to cleanse and charge them properly, then set your intentions.

Suppose you feel an attack and don't have your crystals on you. In that case, you can visualize a circle of light shielding you from unwanted energies. As you do so, guard your stomach and legs by covering them. You can cross your arms and legs or put a pillow on your stomach. These are easy ways to shield yourself until you wear your crystals or remove yourself from the situation altogether.

Spirit Guide Communication

According to spiritualists, every person was assigned a spirit team before birth. It is said that before your arrival on Earth, you were a soul in the spirit realm. You agreed to or chose to go back to earth in that realm. Before your spirit entered into your ego, it agreed to a contract with other spirits. In this pact, you and your spirit guides agreed to take this journey together. You were sent to Earth to accomplish your spirit's mission, and your spirit team will look after you.

Your spirit team loves you unconditionally and is always looking out for you. They are there for you in times of need, sending love, support, and blessings your way. Since your spirit team wants the best for you, getting their views and opinions will be interesting and enriching.

We often wish there was someone to guide us and help us find the right answers in life. If you've felt this way before, you don't need to keep wishing and wondering. You can simply ask your spirit guides.

You can communicate with your spirit guides in numerous ways. This section will explore communicating with your spirit team using the pendulum. This may sound daunting, but it really isn't. Once you talk to them, you'll feel at ease and at home. Here's what you need to get started.

First, find a comfortable spot in your home. It could be your meditation spot or next to your altar. Next, create a board and write down the following words: "yes," "no," and "maybe." If you don't want to create one, you can easily find one online. Remember that communicating with your spirit team is a deeply personal matter, so your board can have whatever you like on it. It could have other words and doesn't have to contain the standard answers. You can personalize this as much as you want.

With your board ready, you can finally grab your pendulum and connect with your spirit guides. You can get to know them, ask them questions, or talk to them about life and heed their advice.

After you've finished talking to your guides, thank them for your conversation. Keeping up communication with your team is always a good idea. Maintaining a relationship with your spirit team, who love and care for you, can be very soul-rewarding.

Past-Life Reading

If you believe in reincarnation, you know that every soul has experienced different lives over the course of its existence. Naturally, at some point in time, you must have felt curious about your past life. Who were you? Were you a woman or a man? What are your karmic debts? During which era did you live? Is there anyone in your life right now who was also with you in your past life? Did you have karmic relationships in this past life?

Some people would rather not know about their past life, but others do. Ultimately, it all comes down to your intuition. Your higher self will tell you whether it's a good idea to know about your previous life. If you feel the need to know about your past life, or your intuition is guiding you to get in touch with it, then this is a sign that you should explore this part of your soul's journey.

You can use your pendulum to delve back into your past life. Before you begin, you need to have patience, as this is a slow process. To start, write down your questions. Here are a few ideas:

- Was I a woman or a man in my most recent past life?
- Did I have a joyous life?
- Was I a good person?
- Did I fulfill my soul's purpose in my past life?
- Do I know anyone now from my past life?
- Do I have karmic relationships in this current life?
- How many times have I been reincarnated?

When asking the pendulum about your date of birth, be as specific as possible. For example, ask if you were born in the 18th, 19th, or 20th century. You can ask about each decade to know more. You can do the same with countries or continents, in which case you should get a map and see where your pendulum takes you. There is an infinity of things you can ask the pendulum about. Brainstorm and ask any question that stimulates your curiosity and that you feel brings you closer to your deeper spiritual self.

Numerous practitioners are concerned about their karmic debts, so they try to get as much information about it from their reading. Karmic debts are actions that you took in a past life. These actions may have caused an imbalance in your karma, meaning you'll have to make amends for it in your next life. If you feel preoccupied with your karmic debt, you might want to ask your pendulum about it.

Readers also ask about their karmic relationships. Karmic relationships involve people who knew each other in a past life. During their time together in their past life, they experienced obstacles that stood in the way of their growth. As a result, they meet again in their next life to make amends and grow together in their relationship.

Here are some questions you can ask your pendulum: Do I have karmic debts? What are they? Can I repay them in this life? How can I repay them? Do I have karmic relations in this life? Why? Who do I have a karmic relationship with?

Remember that the pendulum will move differently if you're not using a board, picture, or map. If you're not using any tools, the pendulum will move clockwise for "yes" and anticlockwise for "no."

Numerology

Do you often encounter a pattern of the same number? Have you ever wondered whether it was a coded message for you? Did you wonder why you keep seeing them? If your answer to these questions is "yes," you might be interested in numerology. This ancient divination practice was founded in China, then later popularized in Europe by Pythagoras. The idea behind numerology is that every number has a message of significance behind it. It teaches us that everything around us can be translated into numbers and that these numbers can help unveil coded messages.

Pendulum and Numerology

Many pendulum users combine numerology with pendulum magic. You can use these together to gather insights about the future or better understand synchronicities. While there are various ways to integrate these two practices, you first need to understand the meaning behind each number. The following chart details what each number signifies in numerology:

Number	General meanings
01	• The self • Self-expression • Independence • Innovative
02	• Duality • Equilibrium

	• Justice • Intuition • Supportive • Protective • Inclusive • Empathetic
03	• Left-brain faculties • Communication • Artistic • Optimism • Jovial
04	• Proactive • Patience • Loyalty • Restrictions • Dependable • Conscientious
05	• Love • Freedom of expression • Energetic • Adventurous • Creativity
06	• Healing • Nurturing • Left and right brain • Anxiety • Depression

07	• Analytical • Spiritual • Intellectual • Philosophical
08	• Materialistic • Accomplished • Wisdom
09	• Humanitarian • Sacrifice • Idealism • Responsible

According to occultist Richard Webster, the best way to gather insights about the future with pendulum numerology is to understand what each number represents and decipher its meaning according to the question asked. In other words, you may need to interpret these numbers differently according to your question.

To predict your future using numerology, Webster advises you to get 9 envelopes along with 9 cards. Label the cards from 1 to 9, and assign one card to each envelope. Now, scramble the envelopes until you forget the cards' placements.

As you shuffle the cards, think about your question. Try to be precise with your question – the more detailed, the better. If your question is too broad, then you may get a vague answer.

Place the 9 envelopes in a row and grab your pendulum. Ask your question and watch the pendulum work its magic. Gently hover the pendulum over the envelopes without moving it. Go over each card and observe the pendulum's movements. The pendulum should swing more vividly around a certain envelope, indicating that you have your answer. Now, open your envelope and see which number you have.

Here, you'll find an interpretation for each number to help you figure out an answer to your question.

New beginnings. It's time to be ambitious and show initiative toward your goals. Be patient. This is not the time to push your luck. Sit back, and what you have worked for will reward you. (1)

Be patient. This is not the time to push your luck. Sit back, and what you have worked for will reward you. (2)

Balance is key. It is important to prioritize your personal needs. Set time for work, and set some for playtime and relaxation. (3)

Slow progress. You might be feeling frustrated that your labor hasn't borne any fruit. Remember that growth takes time and that good things come to those who wait. (4)

Transformation. Brace yourself as you are about to experience some kind of change in your life. (5)

It is time to give back. The universe is inviting you to share your love and care with your family and loved ones. (6)

Feed your spirit. Now is the time to meditate, practice grounding, spend time with nature, and nurture your soul. (7)

Material gains. You may have been worrying about your finances lately. There's no need to be anxious. Maintain the balance between work and relaxation, and money will soon come your way. (8)

Replenishing. Now is the time to get rid of what doesn't serve you. Bid farewell to those who aren't good for you and relinquish any habits that don't serve your spiritual growth. (9)

Everyday Magic

As you can see, you can learn many special things from your pendulum. It can give you the kind of answers that would otherwise be impossible to find anywhere else. That said, there are other uses for your cherished tool. Since magic exists everywhere and in everything, you can use your pendulum to learn about things in your everyday life, like retrieving lost objects, checking on your health, and interpreting dreams.

Finding Lost Items

Misplacing an item can be terribly frustrating, especially when you're in a hurry. Luckily, you don't have to spend time scavenging for it or succumb to anxiety. You can simply just ask your pendulum, and it will answer you.

Grab your pendulum and visualize the item you're looking for. Ask the pendulum if your item is located around your house, in your car, at the office, etc. Keep asking your pendulum and wait for an answer. The best way to start is with broad questions, then move on to detailed ones. You can also ask if someone stole it or has "borrowed" it without your knowledge.

You can also do the same with people or pets. For this, get a picture of the person or animal in question. You can also grab a map or a piece of paper with different locations and start asking the pendulum. Many pendulum users do this to help themselves or others when they've lost someone they love. This method can yield effective and fast results if done correctly and with the right intention.

Inquiring about Your Health

It's normal for everyone to worry about their health from time to time. However, when one thinks of their health, their mind goes directly to their physical state. Are they consuming healthy food? Should they follow a new workout routine? Are they taking their medications? While all of these questions are valid, keeping a healthy body is not synonymous with physical well-being.

Your health is composed of mainly four factors: physical, mental, emotional, and spiritual health. Each must be addressed and taken care of properly. Unfortunately, in our modern, fast-paced lives, one can often lose sight of their well-being.

While neglecting your emotional and spiritual health won't kill you, it will certainly make your life challenging. Taking the time to nurture your soul and care for yourself emotionally and mentally will be rewarding beyond imagination.

If you're unsure about your health status, you can ask your pendulum. You can ask which of the four factors requires the most attention. Which parts need nourishment and extra care? The answer may surprise you. Once you can get straight answers to simple questions, you can ask your pendulum for ways to take care of your soul. How can you bolster your emotional health? What is the best way to heal yourself mentally? You can set a day where you take care of your needs. Again, seeking answers from your pendulum should never be a substitute for a medical check-up with a health professional.

In parallel to your pendulum practice, you can learn more about your mental health with self-help books or by going to therapy. You can get a massage once a month. You can meditate and practice breathing exercises to feed your spirit. You can also attune to your emotions and feelings by journaling and spending some of your time in nature.

Dreams

Many people focus on their dream work for a variety of reasons. Most believe that the subconscious speaks to them through their dreams. Others believe that dreams transport them to a different realm or an alternative life. Some even like to write down their dreams to practice lucid dreaming and astral projection. If you're as interested in your dreams as these people are, you may want to start paying more attention to them.

If you haven't done this before, then you may wake up forgetting your dreams or remembering them by chance. To keep track of your dreams, you should start journaling. This will help you remember your dreams more vividly. However, this method isn't completely error-proof. If you wake up one day and forget your dreams, you can always ask your pendulum about them.

Before you ask your pendulum, try to remember how your dream felt. This will help you narrow down your questions. You can then start with broad questions: was it a good dream or a bad one? What were you doing in the dream? Here, you can list down different activities (watching TV, cooking, working out, or even flying). Was there anyone with you in the dream? Did it have a coded spiritual message? What should you learn from this dream?

After you've finished with your questions, journal about your experience with the pendulum. Write down your questions and describe the pendulum's movements. This will help you progress and hone your craft when it comes to using your pendulum.

All in all, pendulum magic is exceptionally useful and versatile. It's one of the rare tools you can easily integrate with other divination practices to give you answers to anything you inquire about.

As you've seen, you can use your pendulum to protect yourself energetically. You can ask if you are being energetically attacked and which tools you need to protect yourself spiritually. You can also communicate with your spirit guides using the pendulum. You'll see how easily the conversation flows between you, especially when you're around such loving and nurturing spirits.

The pendulum can also help paint a picture of your past life. All you need to do is narrow down your questions and write down their answers. You do not have to complete a past life reading in one sit down. This can be done over a few days if you like. Incorporating numerology into your pendulum reading could give you a richer insight. Pendulum magic is a vast world; there are numerous magical rituals that you can try for yourself. Some activities are mentioned here, but you can also branch out by practicing other ones. Finally, you can practice magic daily by asking about lost items, health, and dreams.

Conclusion

Despite the plethora of divination tools being used today, pendulums are and continue to be the most popular ones throughout history. This is due to their straightforward usage and easy techniques. Divination practices open up your mind to a vast, unexplored world. Once you open yourself up to this soulful practice, you'll be able to explore your psychic powers to understand different aspects and viewpoints of life. You'll see the world with a new pair of eyes once you master the art of pendulum magic. An older version of you would be surprised at the decisions you may make once you start allowing your intuition to guide you toward success.

Using your pendulum to explore different paths in your life will certainly prove helpful. This way, you can attune yourself to your intuition and get nudged toward the right answers in life. While it is sometimes challenging to trust your intuition, opening yourself up to this new level of wisdom might be just what will guide you in the right direction. Once you connect with your pendulum, know for certain that it will be a lifelong friend to you. Even years after they've worn out and broken down, they will be a memory of all the good decisions you made.

When using the pendulum, you must show trust, patience, and perseverance to obtain successful results. And while you might not always get the correct predictions or outcomes you expected, losing hope in this practice is not the way forward. So, move slowly and lovingly in this practice. Soon enough, you'll become a master of pendulum magic, taking readings for your friends and loved ones. Make sure you practice it regularly, and do not be tempted to give up if it's not working. Perhaps you just need a change of mind, a change of scenery, or a change of heart to get better results.

It's also important that you don't compare your pendulum journey with those of others. This is something everyone will experience in their own unique way. Know that there is no right or wrong way to use the pendulum. Simply remember what you've learned from this book and other resources, and you'll master different pendulum techniques in no time. Get your pendulums out and create a magical connection between your pendulums and your self-intuition.

Make sure you select a pendulum that has sparked something in you. Embrace this divination tool as something you love and care for; soon enough, you'll feel a bond so strong that it will be unbreakable. This connection may or may not change your entire life, but it will give you genuinely good advice whenever you need it. Take all the help you can get from this book, apply all your knowledge to practical techniques, and witness real change in your life. Always remember that the results obtained from these techniques aren't set in stone and that the final decision will always depend on you. Good luck!

Here's another book by Silvia Hill that you might like

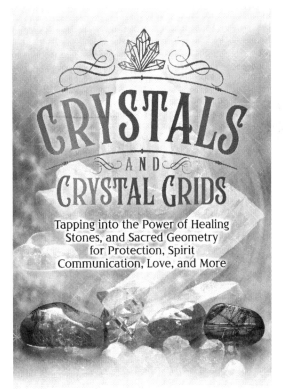

CRYSTALS
AND
CRYSTAL GRIDS

Tapping into the Power of Healing
Stones, and Sacred Geometry
for Protection, Spirit
Communication, Love, and More

SILVIA HILL

Free Bonus from Silvia Hill available for limited time

Hi Spirituality Lovers!

My name is Silvia Hill, and first off, I want to THANK YOU for reading my book.

Now you have a chance to join my exclusive spirituality email list so you can get the ebooks below for free as well as the potential to get more spirituality ebooks for free! Simply click the link below to join.

P.S. Remember that it's 100% free to join the list.

~~$27~~ FREE BONUSES

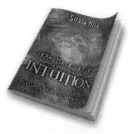

 9 Types of Spirit Guides and How to Connect to Them

 How to Develop Your Intuition: 7 Secrets for Psychic Development and Tarot Reading

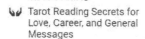 Tarot Reading Secrets for Love, Career, and General Messages

Access your free bonuses here
https://livetolearn.lpages.co/pendulum-for-beginners-paperback/

References

Desy, P. L. (n.d.). What is Dowsing? Learn Religions. https://www.learnreligions.com/what-is-dowsing-1731451

Oakes, J. (2021, September 21). How To Use A Pendulum: The A-Z Guide. Tiny Rituals. https://tinyrituals.co/blogs/tiny-rituals/how-to-use-a-pendulum

Webster, R. (2002). Pendulum magic for beginners: Power to achieve all goals. Llewellyn Publications.

Pendulum users from the past. (n.d.). Google.Com. https://sites.google.com/site/westmorlanddowsers/pendulum-users-from-the-past

Tucker, C. (2020, September 7). The History of a Pendulum. Wilde Folk. https://shopwildefolk.com/blogs/news/the-history-of-a-pendulum

Pendulum Dowsing – An Introduction to Using a Pendulum. (n.d.). Holistic Shop. https://www.holisticshop.co.uk/articles/guide-pendulum-dowsing

Barbara. (2015, May 8). Wooden pendulum. Colorful Crafts; Barbara. https://colorful-crafts.com/wooden-pendulum/

Choosing crystals. (n.d.). Thecrystalhealer.co.uk. http://www.thecrystalhealer.co.uk/Crystal-Information/Choosing-Crystals

Mike. (2015, August 17). Different pendulums and their uses. Instant Karma Asheville. https://www.instantkarmaasheville.com/different-pendulums-and-their-uses/

Wigington, P. (2009, March 17). Learn to use a pendulum for divination. Learn Religions. https://www.learnreligions.com/pendulum-divination-2561760

Abundance Mindset Mama. (2021, July 1). How to cleanse A pendulum-5 easy ways. Abundance Mindset Mama. https://abundancemindsetmama.com/how-to-cleanse-a-pendulum

Huberman, L. (2020, September 6). How to charge + cleanse a pendulum. Ark Made. https://ark-made.com/blogs/guides/how-to-charge-cleanse-a-pendulum

Julia. (2017, June 24). Pendulums 101: how to cleanse, program, and care for your pendulum. Julia North. https://julianorth.co/blog/2017/06/pendulums-101-cleansing-programming-and-caring-for-your-pendulum

p-themes. (n.d.). Cleansing & charging. Cinnabar Soul. https://cinnabarsoul.com/collections/cleansing-charging/pendulum

Samantha. (2020, February 28). How to cleanse A pendulum: 5 strong & easy ways. Tea & Rosemary. https://teaandrosemary.com/cleanse-pendulum/

Ask Your Pendulum. (n.d.). How to use a pendulum. Ask Your Pendulum. https://askyourpendulum.com/pages/how-to-use-a-pendulum

Cleansing, charging, and programming your pendulum. (n.d.). The Angel's Medium. https://www.theangelsmedium.com/programming-your-pendulum

Creating your own Sacred Space in your Home. (n.d.). NATALIA KUNA | Intuitive, Healer | Creator of Spiritual Course Academy. https://www.nataliakuna.com/creating-your-own-sacred-space.html

How to program your pendulum. (2019, May 16). FreerSpirit Akashic Soul Readings. https://freerspirit.com/2019/05/16/how-to-program-your-pendulum/

Voss, S. (2019, July 3). Creating a Sacred Space using Crystal Energy. Earth Family Crystals. https://earthfamilycrystals.com/blogs/default-blog/creating-a-sacred-space-using-crystal-energy

A beginner's guide to 10 types of crystals & how to use each of them. (2021, May 12). Mindbodygreen. https://www.mindbodygreen.com/articles/types-of-crystals

Ashley. (2021, November 18). 6 of the best crystal pendulums to have. Moon of Gemini. https://moonofgemini.com/crystal-pendulums/

Caroline, E. (2021, May 17). Crystals for chakra healing. Ohana; Ohana Yoga + Barre. https://ohanayoga.com/crystals-for-chakra-healing/

CASTLE MARKETING. (2019, October 4). Grounding with crystals. Crystal Castle. https://www.crystalcastle.com.au/grounding-with-crystals/

Estrada, J. (2021, February 16). 10 types of crystals for healing, self-love, energy clearing, and positivity. Well+Good. https://www.wellandgood.com/types-crystals/

Keithley, Z. (2022, June 15). 7 grounding crystals and stones for stability & protection. Zanna Keithley. https://zannakeithley.com/grounding-crystals-and-stones/

Lindberg, S. (2020, August 24). What are chakras? Meaning, location, and how to unblock them. Healthline. https://www.healthline.com/health/what-are-chakras

Mike. (2015, August 17). Different pendulums and their uses. Instant Karma Asheville. https://www.instantkarmaasheville.com/different-pendulums-and-their-uses/

Owen, N. (2020, April 21). Healing crystals guide: the best crystals for you and how to use them. Cosmopolitan. https://www.cosmopolitan.com/uk/worklife/a32144127/healing-crystals/

Palermo, E., & Gordon, J. (2022, January 25). Crystal healing: Stone-cold facts about gemstone treatments. Livescience.com; Live Science. https://www.livescience.com/40347-crystal-healing.html

Rekstis, E. (2022, January 21). Everything you need to know about healing crystals and their benefits. Healthline. https://www.healthline.com/health/mental-health/guide-to-healing-crystals

Roots, A. (n.d.). Seven Chakra Pendulum. Angelic Roots. https://www.angelicroots.com/products/seven-chakra-pendulum

Scoop, S. (2022, June 1). 25 best crystals to use for grounding and healing energy. Sarah Scoop. https://sarahscoop.com/25-best-crystals-to-use-for-grounding-and-healing-energy/

Sylvester, M. (2022, June 30). These are the best crystals for each chakra. Nylon. https://www.nylon.com/life/crystals-for-each-chakra

The science behind healing crystals explained! (2019, August 1). The Times of India; Times Of India. https://timesofindia.indiatimes.com/life-style/health-fitness/home-remedies/the-science-behind-healing-crystals-explained/articleshow/70482968.cms

Veronese, L. (2022, June 23). A complete guide to the best crystals for each chakra. Hello Glow. https://helloglow.co/crystals-for-chakras/

Walters, M. (2021, September 17). Are healing crystals for real? Here's what the science says. Healthline. https://www.healthline.com/health/healing-crystals-what-they-can-do-and-what-they-cant

We Thieves, C. (2019, September 9). An introduction to crystals and their healing properties. We Thieves.

What are chakras? (n.d.). WebMD. https://www.webmd.com/balance/what-are-chakras

Zoldan, R. J. (2020, June 22). Your 7 chakras, explained—plus, how to tell if they're blocked. Well+Good. https://www.wellandgood.com/what-are-chakras/

Pendulum Dowsing – An Introduction to Using a Pendulum. (n.d.). Holistic Shop. https://www.holisticshop.co.uk/articles/guide-pendulum-dowsing

Davis, F. (2021, July 22). Dowsing With a Pendulum: What It Is, How It Works & How To Do It. Cosmic Cuts. https://cosmiccuts.com/blogs/healing-stones-blog/dowsing-with-a-pendulum

Aletheia. (2017, December 18). How to Use a Dowsing Pendulum For Divination - Beginner's Guide ★. LonerWolf. https://lonerwolf.com/dowsing-pendulum/

Store, E. M. W. (2021, April 24). How to Use a Pendulum for Divination. East Meets West USA. https://www.eastmeetswestusa.com/blogs/east-meets-west-blog-articles/how-to-use-a-pendulum-for-divination

Davis, F. (2021, July 22). Dowsing With a Pendulum: What It Is, How It Works & How To Do It. Cosmic Cuts. https://cosmiccuts.com/blogs/healing-stones-blog/dowsing-with-a-pendulum

Kinsey, E. (n.d.). What is divination: a beginners guide. Spirit and Destiny. https://www.spiritanddestiny.co.uk/wellbeing-and-mindfulness/spirituality/what-is-divination/

Kinsey, E. (n.d.). What is a pendulum and how to use it for guidance or spiritual healing. Spirit and Destiny. https://www.spiritanddestiny.co.uk/wellbeing-and-mindfulness/spirituality/what-is-a-pendulum/

Ask Your Pendulum. (n.d.-a). How to use pendulum charts. Ask Your Pendulum. https://askyourpendulum.com/pages/how-to-use-pendulum-charts

Ask Your Pendulum. (n.d.-b). How to use your pendulum with a multiple choice chart. Ask Your Pendulum. https://askyourpendulum.com/pages/how-to-use-your-pendulum-with-a-multiple-choice-chart

Paige, A. (2009, April 9). How to make a pendulum chart. Synonym.com; Synonym. https://classroom.synonym.com/how-to-make-a-pendulum-chart-12078741.html

Pendulum dowsing manual guide + free sample pendulum charts. (n.d.). Abundance Belief. https://abundancebelief.com/product/pendulum-dowsing-manual-free-sample-charts/

Use a pendulum chart * Wicca-spirituality.com. (n.d.). Wicca-spirituality.com https://www.wicca-spirituality.com/pendulum-chart.html

A beginner's guide to the 7 chakras. (2009, October 28). Mindbodygreen. https://www.mindbodygreen.com/articles/7-chakras-for-beginners

Ask Your Pendulum. (n.d.). How to use your pendulum to check the status of your chakras. Ask Your Pendulum. https://askyourpendulum.com/pages/how-to-use-your-pendulum-to-check-the-status-of-your-chakras

Energy Work With Pendulums, Crystals, and Reiki (2013) - Lynn Marie Gravatt. (n.d.). Scribd. https://www.scribd.com/document/346157723/energy-work-with-pendulums-crystals-and-reiki-2013-lynn-marie-gravatt

How to balance your chakras with a pendulum. (n.d.). Gaia. https://www.gaia.com/article/how-balance-your-chakras-pendulum

Hughes, L. (2019, March 1). What are healing crystals and do they actually work? Oprah Daily. https://www.oprahdaily.com/life/health/a26559820/healing-crystals/

Shah, P. (2020, August 20). A primer of the chakra system. Chopra. https://chopra.com/articles/what-is-a-chakra

What is Reiki, and Does it Really Work? (2021, August 30). Cleveland Clinic. https://health.clevelandclinic.org/reiki/

7 Ways to Strengthen Your Intuition Muscle. (n.d.). Byrdie. https://www.byrdie.com/how-to-strengthen-your-intuition-muscle-5186284

Coughlin, S. (n.d.). We Asked 5 Spiritual Workers To Define "Intuition" — Here's What They Said. Www.refinery29.com. https://www.refinery29.com/en-gb/what-is-intuition-psychic-spiritual-meaning

Highly Intuitive: How Meditation Trains Our Intuition – EOC Institute. (n.d.). Eocinstitute.org. from https://eocinstitute.org/meditation/develop-your-intuition-through-meditation/

Third Eye Chakra Stones: 15 Must-Have Crystals For The Ajna. (n.d.). Tiny Rituals. https://tinyrituals.co/blogs/tiny-rituals/third-eye-chakra-stones

Visualization Meditation: 5 Exercises to Try. (2020, May 28). Healthline. https://www.healthline.com/health/visualization-meditation#:~:text=When%20you%20visualize%2C%20you%20focus

Number 9 Meaning in Numerology. (n.d.). Www.numerology.com. https://www.numerology.com/articles/about-numerology/single-digit-number-9-meaning/

Phillips, D. A. (2015). The complete book of numerology: discovering the inner self. Hay House.

Webster, R. (2002). Pendulum magic for beginners: power to achieve all goals. Llewellyn Publication

---

Made in the USA
Columbia, SC
16 November 2024

46718182R00072